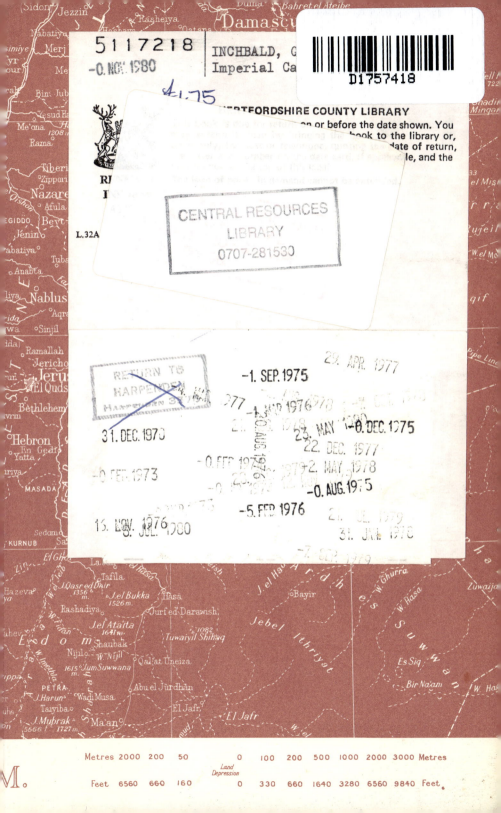

Metres 2000 200   50   0   100 200 500 1000 2000 3000 Metres

                        Land
                     Depression

Feet 6560 660 160   0   330 660 1640 3280 6560 9840 Feet

IMPERIAL CAMEL CORPS

Chapter Two

THE IMPERIAL CAMEL CORPS

AT THE END of 1915 Lieutenant-Colonel Leslie Smith, a splendid
and gallant soldier who had already served for twenty years in
the Middle East and had won a V.C. in Somaliland some years
before, decided, in view of the immense difficulties encountered
by the cavalry in maintaining the various outposts and carrying
out the constant patrolling which was required throughout
thousands of square miles of virtually waterless desert, to approach
General Sir John Maxwell, who was at that time G.O.C.-in-C.
Egyptian Expeditionary Force, for permission to raise a white-
man camel corps composed entirely of officers and men recruited
from mounted units. This corps was to be a self contained and
completely independent fighting force to take over the job of
patrolling and maintaining contact with the Senussi in the vast
desert areas to the west of the Nile Valley and the north of
the Sudan.

At first this proposal was not well received. For one thing
he was told that white men could not handle camels and that he
would have to recruit native troops, and for another he met
with strong opposition from the officers commanding cavalry
regiments, who not unreasonably resented the idea of their
units being used as reserves for the proposed camel corps. These
were nearly all regular or ex-regular officers to whom it was
almost an insult to mention camels in the same breath with
horses and, even when permission was finally obtained, and the
new corps had come into being as the Imperial Camel Corps

and already begun to more than justify itself as a fighting force, they persisted in their belief that it was no more than a glorified labour corps. In fact it was often confused with the Egyptian Camel Corps and even more so with the Camel Transport Corps which, although officered by British officers, was in reality a native unit used exclusively for the transport of the vast quantities of water and supplies required for the upkeep of the armies in the field including, I may say, the dozens of cavalry regiments scattered throughout the waterless wastes in which they had to operate. Incidentally the Camel Transport Corps was afterwards to do a magnificent job and play a vital part in Allenby's campaigns for the conquest of Palestine. I have a vivid recollection of the time after the capture of Beersheba when the forward troops ran out of water and we lay all day under a burning sun without a drop to drink, nor so far as we could see any hope of one, and the arrival late that evening of a large convoy of camels carrying sufficient water for the needs of something like three divisions. I am not exaggerating when I say that it was touch and go whether we should be able to continue.

The first units of the Imperial Camel Corps were derived from the Australian and New Zealand mounted regiments and in due course they made up the 1st, 3rd and 4th Battalions. But my story is concerned with the 2nd Battalion, which was formed in the early months of 1916 and derived almost entirely from British Yeomanry regiments, although later on a company (No. 5) was added from an infantry division. This company was part of a force, under the command of Colonel S. F. Newcombe, who had played a leading part in Lawrence's raiding operations against the Hejaz railway. The force was employed in sabotage work behind the Turkish lines at Beersheba but eventually came to grief when it was surrounded and captured by the enemy, after losing more than half its men killed or wounded.

CONTENTS

LIST OF ILLUSTRATIONS

Between pages 62 and 63

F 15.

ACKNOWLEDGEMENTS

THE PHOTOGRAPH of the Memorial to the Imperial Camel Corps is reproduced by kind permission of Mr Herbert Whytehead, who served in the same Company as myself, and I am grateful to Mrs Reginald Maffett for allowing me to use the photograph of her brother, the late Baron Alan de Rutzen, and lending me her only copy for the purpose.

My thanks are due to Jonathan Cape Limited and the Executors of the T. E. Lawrence Estate for leave to reproduce two of the maps contained in *Seven Pillars of Wisdom* in addition to a quotation from the text, and also to Mr William Roberts, R.A. who has very kindly allowed me to use his drawing of the late Lieutenant-Colonel R. V. Buxton, D.S.O., which appears in the 1935 edition of the same work. I am also grateful to John Bartholomew & Son Limited for their permission to reproduce sections from two of the maps contained in the *Great World Atlas* published by the Reader's Digest Association. One of these is shown in the endpapers.

I acknowledge with gratitude the great assistance I have received from Mr Laurence Moore, M.B.E., Wing Commander C. H. N. Ashlin, and also from Captain J. A. Lyall, M.C., all of whom served with the Imperial Camel Corps in several of its campaigns. Without their help I should never have been able to give the complete story of the Camel Corps which I have endeavoured to do in this book. Mr Moore, in particular, has been unremitting in his efforts to provide me both from his own experiences and the material, which he has gathered over the years, with details of the Hejaz Campaign and the operations which took place in what I have called the Southern Oases, while Wing Commander Ashlin's account of the Battle of Romani and subsequent operations in Sinai has proved invaluable.

I also have to thank Mr Percy Pritchard, A.R.P.S. for placing at my disposal various photographs and contemporary press cuttings. I have reproduced three of the former, which were taken from a captured German officer, and the latter have been of great help to me in my description of the engagements at Maghdaba and Rafa. I acknowledge the assistance I have received from *A Popular History of the Great War*, edited by Sir J. A. Hammerton and published in the years succeeding the 1914–1918 War, in building up part of the historical background, and also the kindness of Dr Christopher Dowling and Mr V. Rigby in allowing me access to certain books and papers held by the Imperial War Museum.

I owe a particular debt of gratitude to Mrs Theodora Duncan of Los Angeles who has not only taken a great interest in the preparation of this book but also given me considerable assistance in the form of photographs and other material from ' The Theodora Duncan Collection of T. E. Lawrence ', which she has kindly permitted me to use, also to Mr Lowell Thomas for allowing me to quote extensively from the revised and enlarged edition, published in the U.S.A. in 1967, of his well-known book *With Lawrence in Arabia*, which first appeared nearly fifty years ago.

In conclusion I would like to offer my grateful acknowledgements to Mr Peter Giddy for his continual interest and practical advice, to Mr Norman Haynes for the time and trouble which he has devoted to the production of this book and to my wife for again spending so many uncomplaining hours at her typewriter.

FOREWORD

THE STORY which I related in my previous book *Camels and Others* of the adventures of the Imperial Camel Corps in Egypt, Sinai, Palestine and Trans-Jordania throughout 1916, 1917 and 1918 was incomplete in two very important respects, namely its first engagement which was fought in August 1916 to the east of the Suez Canal and came to be known as the Battle of Romani, and its final operations which took place in 1918 when some 300 men and 400 camels were lent by General Allenby to Lawrence for participation, in conjunction with his Arabs, in the campaign he was planning against the Turkish forces which were still sitting astride and to the east of the Hejaz Railway. The object of the present book is to rectify these omissions and to concentrate in one small volume a detailed and consecutive account of the activities of the Imperial Camel Corps as they developed throughout the three years of its existence.

Following the publication of *Camels and Others* I had the good fortune to establish contact with Mr Laurence (Rory) Moore, M.B.E. of Leeds, who not only served with the Imperial Camel Corps throughout the whole of its existence and for most of the time as N.C.O. i/c Signals with 2nd Battalion H.Q. (this Battalion comprised the whole of the British as distinct from the Australian and New Zealand contingents) but also took an active part in the Hejaz operations, and he has very kindly supplied me, for inclusion in this book, with an account of the latter which is based on a series of lectures which he has given to various Rotary Clubs over the last two or three years. And this is not all. Mr Moore has played the chief part in maintaining in Yorkshire and the North Midlands an Imperial Camel Corps Old Comrades Association of which he is the Honorary Secretary, and from time to time he publishes a News

Letter which he distributes to the various survivors, and it is surprising how many there still are, with whom he has retained or established contact over the years.

One of these survivors is Wing Commander C. H. N. Ashlin of Chiddingfold, who was wounded at Romani, and to whose kindness I am indebted for permission also to include an account of the operations based on one which he wrote some years ago, and I think I am justified in saying that the material which has been provided from these and other sources, when added to the account which I have already given in *Camels and Others*, makes up a fairly complete history of the Imperial Camel Corps from its inception in the early part of 1916 to its disbandment in 1919 a few months after the final surrender of the Turkish armies. I am, of course, referring to the 2nd Battalion. The 'Deeds and Misdeeds', to quote the author, of the Australian and New Zealand contingents were described in a book called *The Cameliers* by Oliver Hogue (who wrote under the *nom de plume* of Trooper Bluegum) which was published in London in 1919 by Andrew Melrose Ltd.

In order, however, to preserve the continuity of the narrative, and to present the events of which it is made up in their proper perspective and chronological order, I have been compelled to introduce some of the experiences which I have already related in *Camels and Others* and for this repetition I can only express my apologies. I am also including, in addition to a certain amount of historical background, several maps which should help the reader to a better understanding of the different operations in which the Imperial Camel Corps became involved and the enormous areas, parts of which were virtually unmapped, over which they were extended. Before, however, embarking on the story, which begins in the opening months of 1915 with the campaign against the Senussi in the Libyan or Western Desert, I propose to make a few comments of a general nature on the subject of that truly extraordinary creature the camel, who is after all the central figure and indeed the hero of the events which I have to relate.

As a start I would like to explain that there are two completely different species of camel, namely the two humped Asian or Bactrian camel and the one humped Arabian. The Bactrian is larger but has shorter legs and a much thicker coat, which grows longer in winter and enables it to withstand without apparent discomfort the rigours of virtually Siberian conditions. The Arabian is generally spoken of as a dromedary, although the name properly belongs to a special breed of trotting camel like those which were supplied to us from Upper Egypt and the Sudan. Opinions differ as regards loads, distances and speeds but a good dromedary can certainly keep going for twenty-five or even thirty miles a day for weeks on end and at a speed, varying in accordance with conditions and the particular type of camel, from about four to ten miles an hour with a load of 450 lbs or more including the rider. The normal trotting speed, and this is the most comfortable for the rider, is six miles an hour. The speed of a camel can be accurately determined from its tracks.

The hump, which constitutes a reserve of fat, varies in size according to conditions and grows smaller after days of hardship and indifferent food. We were, I remember, under the impression that a camel had four stomachs but this is not correct. The stomach does, however, have a number of separate compartments or pouches each of which carries up to two gallons of a fluid mixture of food and water and this, combined with the ability to subsist on a limited quantity of food, enables the camel to keep going without water for up to five or, if well broken in, six days even under extreme desert conditions, provided that it is not unduly pressed. The swifter breeds can go even faster and further. The sole of the foot, which unites the two toes, is calloused and there are also callosities on the chest and joints, that is to say whatever parts of the body touch racing, and considerable sums of money turn on the results of these grim and savage contests which often end in the death of the vanquished.

None the less, even if beneath the surface some camels may retain a degree of obstinacy and bad temper, domestication although accepted somewhat grudgingly does produce in the main a degree of docility which has been described somewhere, a little unfairly I think, as ' more the result of habitual nonchalance than any outcome of intelligent subservience ' !

God only knows what they thought of us, but we certainly thought a lot of them and after all there were occasions when our lives were in their hands or rather in their humps. Incidentally a camel's usefulness has no limits even though it may be dead. Its flesh, provided that, in accordance with good Moslem practice, it has been slaughtered with the knife, is eaten by the Arabs, who seemed to materialise from nowhere whenever one of ours was dying, the milk of the cows, which is good and nutritious, is drunk or made into butter or cheese, its dung is often the only fuel available in parts of the desert, its skin can be tanned into leather and its hair can be woven into various fabrics or used in the manufacture of artists' brushes. So called camel hair brushes are not, however, always derived from this source. Altogether it is indeed a wonderful and unique creature and we came to have a great affection for our comrades in arms.

Chapter One

THE SENUSSI WAR

THE SENUSSI were a powerful sect of religious fanatics somewhat similar to the Touaregs of the Sahara. They were despotically ruled by descendants in direct line of Sidi Mohammed ben Ali es Senussi, who in turn claimed direct descent from the Prophet Mohammed, and had founded the sect in 1835. These Chiefs combined the functions of supreme ruler and religious head of the sect and their followers believed them to be specially selected by the Prophet, with Allah's approval, to be their spiritual and temporal guide.

The headquarters of the sect were originally at Alexandria but Sidi Mohammed's son and successor, Senussi el Mahdi, established himself in the Kufra Oasis in the Libyan Desert. On his death in 1902 his son, Sidi Idris (who has recently been deposed from the throne of Libya) was too young to succeed, and his nephew, Sidi Ahmed, known as the Grand Senussi, became the Chief. Sidi Ahmed had ambitions to establish himself as the ruler of a great Libyan state. He had always maintained good relations with Egypt but, when Turkey came into the war on the side of Germany, an effort was made to induce Sidi Ahmed to proclaim a Jehad or Holy War against the Allies with the object of inflaming religious fanaticism in Egypt and embarrassing those countries which had Mahomedan subjects.

To this end a Turk, Nuri Bey, was sent early in 1915 as an emissary to Sidi Ahmed with instructions to endeavour to embroil him with the British, who had built a motor road westward along the coast from the railhead at Dabaa to Mersa Matruh, Sidi Barrani and Sollum, about 300 miles to the west of Alexandria, where a small frontier post had been established and was protected by a couple of gunboats operating in the Gulf.

At some distance inland there rose the waterless and virtually unexplored escarpment of the great Libyan Plateau, which extends in a wide semi-circle from the vicinity of Matruh to Sollum and stretches as far south as the remote oasis of Siwa, which had by now been established as the forward headquarters of the Senussi. The British position was, therefore, one of some strength and the Senussi, encamped near Sollum but without artillery, realised that as long as the British maintained command of the sea it was useless for them to attack the posts along the road.

To digress for a moment, Siwa had been considered a Holy City for centuries and was in ancient times the seat of the Oracle of Jupiter Ammon and later the home and burial place of the greatly venerated Oracle and Saint, Sidi Suliman. Although I was to become very familiar with Mersa Matruh and Sollum, and also the oasis of Baharia further to the south, my company, unlike other units of the Imperial Camel Corps, never reached Siwa which has been described as being unlike any other place in the world. It seems that the town resembles from a distance an ancient castle towering above a forest of waving palms. The original site was on the side of two immense limestone rocks which rise steeply from the level of the plain. As the population increased more and more houses were built on top of the old ones and the town, instead of spreading, began to ascend in the air, house upon house and street over street, until it became more like a beehive than anything else. Fathers built houses for their sons on top of their own until, as can be imagined, their great-grandchildren reached really dizzy heights! In the course of time the inside of the town became a vast warren connected by steep twisting tunnels, narrow and dark, rather like galleries in a coal mine. Although, of course, things are very different today it can be said that prior to the First War very few Christians entered Siwa and came out alive.

However, to return to the British at Sollum, their situation was seriously affected in November, 1915, when an Austrian submarine torpedoed a British armed merchantman, the *Tara*, from which only three of the ten boats it carried succeeded in getting away. These were taken in tow by the submarine and their occupants handed over as prisoners of the Senussi. They

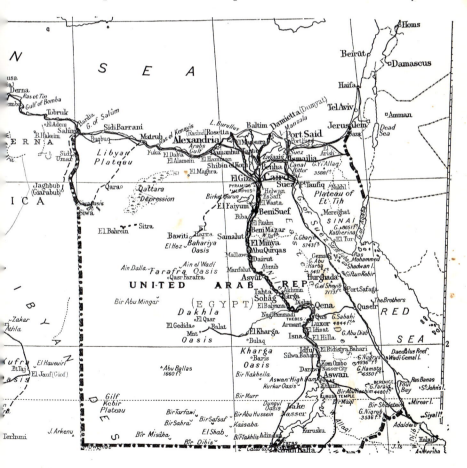

were marched 150 miles into the desert and, as afterwards
transpired, received very bad treatment before being rescued in
March, 1916, by the Duke of Westminster, who was later
awarded the D.S.O., and his squadron of armoured cars which
had only just returned from a very successful encounter with a
large force of Senussi, which they had almost completely
destroyed, including no less than thirty Turkish officers killed or
wounded.

After sinking the *Tara*, the submarine attacked Sollum and
managed to convoy to the shore a steamer on which were about
300 Turkish soldiers, some Turkish and German officers and a
considerable supply of machine guns and ammunition.   They
reached the Senussi camp, and a few days later an attack was
made on the little British force.   The first assault was repulsed
but, as the troops at Sollum were at a great distance from the
railhead at Dabaa, in a rough country and with communications
which could easily be cut by the enemy, it was decided for
strategic and political reasons to withdraw them to Mersa
Matruh, about 180 miles west of Alexandria.

The country round Matruh was valuable on account of the
light sandy soil which produced on the edge of the desert a
bountiful supply of barley, which formed the main food supply
of the Bedouin in the Western Desert and it was certain, therefore,
that if the Senussi seriously intended to undertake any operations
against Egypt, they would first of all endeavour to recover the
barley fields.   To provide against this contingency a strong
column was assembled near Dabaa ready to reinforce the troops
at Matruh.   Aerial reconnaissance showed that the Senussi were
gathering in force from the south and moving eastward.   There
were some patrol encounters with the enemy advance guards,
armed with machine guns, which although inconclusive in
themselves disclosed that a Senussi army of some 5000 men was
gradually collecting in the region of Jebel Medwa near Matruh.

To meet this threat a force was assembled, partly by the

railway and road connecting Alexandria and Matruh and partly by sea transport, consisting of a composite infantry brigade, a composite cavalry brigade and a regiment of Sikhs, who were in fact the only fully trained troops. After spending some days in digging trenches, erecting barbed wire entanglements and generally strengthening the defences, the British commander, Major-General A. Wallace, decided to attack on Christmas Day. Contact was soon made with the Senussi outposts by an infantry column consisting of New Zealanders and the Sikhs and supported by some armoured cars, a mountain battery and, from the sea, the six-inch guns of *H.M.S. Clematis*. The attack on the Senussi positions was pressed home with great dash and courage, amd eventually the ridges which they occupied were stormed and the enemy driven into a deep ravine. Here they made a great stand, assisted by a number of caves which provided excellent natural defences. In consequence it took some time before the ravine was cleared. Unfortunately the encircling movement of the cavalry had been foreseen by Jafar Pasha, a Turkish officer of Arab extraction, who was in command of the Senussi forces, and was delayed by his own mounted troops. In the result, although the whole of their stores as well as flocks of sheep, herds of cattle and a number of camels were captured, the main body of the enemy got away and retreated to Halazin, about twenty miles south of Matruh. It was in the course of this engagement that John Ressich, who was an officer in my own regiment, the Berkshire Yeomanry, came to grief when he galloped with the troop he was commanding over the side of a concealed wadi. He was very severely injured but survived. Several of his men were killed or wounded, and what made it all the worse was that after nightfall the Arab women crept out of their hiding places and mutilated some of them.

During the next few weeks both sides were considerably reinforced and, after another somewhat inconclusive engagement, the Senussi withdrew to the vicintiy of Sidi Barrani, where they occupied a strong defensive position on a ridge at Agagia, some fifteen miles to the south. Here they concentrated a force of 8000 men under Nuri Bey, with Jafar Pasha as his second in command. They were well supplied with machine guns under German and Turkish officers, backed by two pieces of artillery. Towards the end of February Major-General W. E. Peyton, who had now taken command of the British forces which had been strengthened by the inclusion of a cavalry brigade, consisting of the Dorset and Bucks Yeomanry regiments, established his advance base at Umgeila, from where it was proposed to make an all out attack on the enemy at Agagia. The battle which followed under the overall command of General Lukin, and which resulted in the complete defeat and rout of the enemy, was distinguished by a charge of the Dorset Yeomanry under Lieutenant-Colonel H. M. Souter in the course of which five officers were shot down and Souter's horse killed under him right in front of Jafar Pasha, who was himself wounded and taken prisoner.

There were several more engagements before Sollum was finally taken, including those in which the Duke of Westminster played such a prominent part with his armoured cars, and the capture of the Madian and Halfaia passes leading up to the top of the escarpment overlooking Sollum Bay, and it is no exaggeration to say that some of the men, particularly the infantry, suffered almost intolerable hardship from the heavy marching, lack of water and tropical heat. None the less the campaign in the north had been virtually completed, although there was still much to be done in the vast areas of desert to the south, including the occupation of the Siwa Oasis, which did not take place until the 5th February, 1917.

Long before then, however, the condition of the country had been reduced to a terrible state. Not a grain of barley, usually grown along the coast, had been raised during the war. The hostile Arabs, once so well fed from their own land, had been living like the *Tara* prisoners before they were rescued, on anything they could find. Many cairns in the desert told the price they had paid for listening to the blandishments of Nuri Bey and Jafar Pasha and their talk of a Holy War. When the tribesmen came in, with their parties of starving, men women and children, there was a repetition of the old story which has occurred on so many fronts and in so many wars, the British soldier went hungry and the native children shared his rations.

Even as late as March, 1917, when I was at Mersa Matruh for the second time, having joined my regiment there exactly a year earlier, I remember seeing some of these pitiful refugees still coming in and stumbling along behind our camels to collect and eat the undigested grains of corn from their droppings, and no British soldier is proof against that sort of thing, particularly when children are the sufferers, however hungry he may be himself. In fact by that time the larger part of the Senussi army and their followers had already been living for months on the biscuits and dried dates brought by British transports and motor trucks to the coastal towns.

'To those who did not return.'

ISBN 0 85307 094 6

Made and Printed in Great Britain by
Morrison & Gibb Ltd.,
London and Edinburgh.
For Johnson Publications Ltd.,
11/14 Stanhope Mews West, London, S.W.7

IMPERIAL
CAMEL CORPS

BY

GEOFFREY INCHBALD

JOHNSON

LONDON

The other five companies were made up as follows:

No. 6 Cheshire, Shropshire, Mongomeryshire and Denbigh-
shire Yeomanries, commanded by Major J. de Knoop and
Baron Alan de Rutzen both of whom were killed in
action in August, 1916, and later by Captain H. R.
Pettit, M.C. and Lieutenant R. Houghton.

No. 7 Scottish Horse and Lanarkshire, Fife and Forfar and
Ayrshire Yeomanries, commanded by Major F. C.
Gregory, M.C., who was killed in action together with
his second-in-command Captain C. M. Q. Orchardson,
M.C. in December, 1917, and later by Captain E. H.
Deas, M.C. and Captain J. J. Bell-Irving. Deas was also
awarded a Bar to his M.C.

No. 8 Royal Bucks Hussars, 2nd County of London Yeomanry
(Westminster Dragoons) and Berkshire and Dorset
Yeomanries, commanded by Captain C. W. Mason-
MacFarlane, who was killed in action in September, 1916,
and later by Captain J. J. Paterson, Major Julian Day,
M.C., Captain H. W. Tredinnick, M.C. and myself.

No. 9 3rd County of London Yeomanry ('Sharpshooters')
and City of London Yeomanry ('Rough Riders'),
commanded by Major the Earl Winterton and later by
Captain A. F. Newsom, who was killed in action in
March, 1918 and Captain Brothers, M.C.

No. 10 East Riding of Yorkshire Imperial Yeomanry ('Wen-
lock's Horse') and Staffordshire and Lincolnshire Yeomanries, commanded by Major T. Bardwell and later
by Lieutenant C. H. N. Ashlin, Captain A. G. Wilkinson
and Captain J. Lyall, M.C.

The Battalion was commanded by Lieutenant-Colonel Gardner
and later by Lieutenant-Colonel R. V. Buxton, D.S.O.

Each company, which was usually commanded by a Major or
Captain and corresponded more or less to a squadron of cavalry,
was divided into four sections of about thirty-five men, each

commanded by a subaltern. Thus when at full strength, and taking into account Headquarters staff, Lewis Gun sections, Medical, Quartermaster, Veterinary and other personnel, there would be a complement for the five companies of approximately thirty officers and 800 N.C.O.s and men, with the best part of 1000 camels. It was only, however, on the rarest occasions, if at all, that the Battalion functioned as a single unit, and it was usual for one or more companies to be serving quite independently of the rest of the Battalion, either on a different sector of the front or even on a different front altogether with perhaps 1000 miles in between.

No, there was nothing usual about the Imperial Camel Corps and if one includes the Australian and New Zealand companies, which after all constituted about three-quarters of its entire strength, to say nothing of a splendid Sikh Mounted Battery from the Hong Kong and Singapore R.G.A., which was attached to us, a sprinkling of volunteers from the Rhodesian Mounted Police, a South African mining prospector who had fought against the British in the Boer War, a fruit grower from the Canadian Rockies, a pearl fisherman from Queensland, a noted polo player from the Argentine, and even an American, all of whom for some reason chose to throw in their lot with us, it can be seen at once that, omitting the American, the entire British Empire was well represented in our ranks!

It must have been this which prompted the authorship of the following poem or doggerel, call it what you will, which appeared on the 1st September, 1917, over the name of 'Corporal Cuss', in the second issue of *Barrak*, the Camel Corps magazine, which was founded and edited by Captain Morgan (probably 'Corporal Cuss' in person) of Brigade Signals. There was only one further issue during the war and it was not until June, 1967, fifty years later, that the fourth issue was published by Laurence Moore, who has since followed it up with nine more. The poem appeared under the heading 'Abbassia', which was

the barracks outside Cairo where we did our training and
which constituted our base.

> From the furthest isles of Orkney
> From the edge of the Sudan
> From the flats of Murrumbidjee,
> Or the purlieus of Japan,
> From amid the waving Pampas,
> Or the banks of Windermere
> They have gathered, gathered, gathered
> To the Huts of Abbassia.
>
> He whose single thought was salmon
> Met the rogue who poached for pearls,
> And the Billjim made a cobber
> Of the darling of the girls:
> The Guardsman and the Terrier,
> The Plutocrat and Peer——
> All are jumbled up together
> In the Huts of Abbassia.
>
> If you seek for information
> On Polo, Maps or Gin,
> Beer, Beauty or Ballistics,
> You can find it all within:
> If you seek the heat of battle
> Or you're finding life too drear——
> Go and join the ' Curse of Egypt '
> In the Huts of Abbassia.

Allowing for a little poetic license this seems to me to have
been a pretty good and accurate description!

Author's note. I have been asked by an American correspondent
to give some more information with regard to the various
military decorations which are referred to in this book.

V.C. stands for Victoria Cross. It is only awarded for
conspicuous gallantry and is open to all ranks.

D.S.O. stands for Distinguished Service Order and is bestowed in recognition of special services in action of commissioned officers in the Navy, Army, Royal Air Force and Mercantile Marine.

M.C. stands for Military Cross and is awarded to Captains, Lieutenants and Warrant Officers (Class I and II) in the Army and Indian and Colonial Forces.

D.C.M. stands for Distinguished Conduct Medal and is awarded to Warrant officers, non-commissioned officers and men of the Army and Royal Air Force for distinguished conduct in the field.

M.M. stands for Military Medal and is awarded to Warrant and non-commissioned officers and men and serving women.

A Bar to a Decoration (including the Distinguished Service Order) may be awarded for additional service.

Chapter Three

ABBASSIA

THE BERKSHIRE YEOMANRY returned to Cairo from Mersa Matruh in April, 1916, and as it was already overstocked with junior officers and I had only been with them for a month I took the opportunity to volunteer for the Imperial Camel Corps, then in the process of formation, and was more than pleased when my application was accepted.

At the end of April we assembled for training at Abbassia Barracks a few miles out of Cairo and were introduced for the first time to our camels, which obviously liked the look of us even less than we liked the look of them. Most of them, however, were really magnificent animals and we could only hope that they were not quite so supercilious as they looked.

By the time training started in earnest it was getting very hot and, as it turned out, this was the beginning of the hottest summer in Egypt for over forty years, and we were to experience temperatures of anything up to 130° in the shade, and that without any shade except perhaps when we were resting during the hottest part of the day, under cover of a ground sheet supported by four slender poles which were continually blowing down.

Having been accustomed to horses, the men very soon got used to riding camels, though later in the war when No. 5 company was formed from an infantry division they had a lot of difficulty. Probably by then the camels were inferior anyway and a really bad camel can be a very unpleasant customer indeed.

One of the worst I remember was a shaggy bull camel, which was sent to us later in the war with a batch of remounts. He wore a muzzle, which made us suspicious from the start, but we did not realise he was a man-eater! One day, when he was being taken from one part of the lines to another, he suddenly attacked his escort, one of whom was knocked to the ground, whereupon the camel knelt on him and, if it had not been for the muzzle, he would certainly have torn out his throat. Fortunately two of the men were carrying picks and did their utmost to smash the camel's head in. At each blow he roared and flung his head back only to return to the recumbent man on which he was still kneeling. After a few minutes of this he decided to call it a day, got up and wandered off on his own, still roaring his head off. It was decided he should be destroyed and, armed with a shotgun, which apparently had no effect whatsoever, and a rifle, the company commander successfully put an end to his activities for good. After that we had quite a number of the same sort and, by a curious coincidence, they were all found to be dead the morning after their arrival. No enquiry was held though it was tacitly understood that a felony had been committed under extreme provocation. After all the men had quite enough to do fighting a war without having to fight their camels as well. In any case animals like this were not only a nuisance but also completely useless.

In the main, however, they were docile enough, though some of them had a nasty habit of suddenly turning their heads round and trying to bite your knees off. Yet, however much they might complain and grumble, and it must be admitted that they spent a lot of time in this way, their powers of endurance and willingness to go on until they literally dropped were quite remarkable. They may have been ill disposed, though I think that appearances were sometimes deceptive, but they were indeed great hearted as I will show later on.

They were also very comfortable to ride, particularly when

trotting. There was no up and down movement, just forward and back, and as we packed the wooden saddles with blankets or sheepskins, there was no discomfort at all even after several hours riding. In this way they kept up a steady six miles an hour almost indefinitely. If you pressed them beyond that they would break into a canter or gallop which was quite horrible, and frequently ended in the rider being thrown. There were no stirrups or reins, simply a rope tied on to the camel's nose and leading back on one side. With this and the pressure of your feet on either side of its shoulder you could guide the animal without any difficulty. Occasionally there were pullers which had to be restrained by a small wooden peg fitted into a nostril and attached to the rider by a separate cord. Generally the slightest pull on this did the trick, which is not surprising considering the pain it must have caused, but in very obstinate cases the nostril used to be terribly torn.

The noise when the camels were mounted was unbelievable. They would be kneeling down and, when the order was given, each man would take hold of his camel by its nose, turn its head towards him, place one foot on its neck and lift himself on to the saddle, and lean well back to counteract the motion of the camel getting up hind legs first. On every single occasion every single camel roared in protest while this was going on and the effect was staggering.

We kept them beautifully clean, at any rate while we were training. It was different later on. There was grooming every morning for at least an hour. The camels were tethered in a hollow square facing inwards, and after the usual washing, combing, scraping and brushing had been completed, accompanied by a continual hissing on the part of the 'groom' which must have astonished the camels, they had to be de-ticked. Camel ticks are unpleasant little beasts, bigger than sheep ticks, and they invariably took up their positions immediately under the camel's tail, where they proceeded to burrow in and gorge themselves so that, if they were left undisturbed for a few hours, you would find that your camel had what looked, at a distance, like a large bunch of grapes hanging down behind. It was very necessary, therefore, to get the ticks out as soon as possible, and at grooming parade little straw fires were made all round the square into which the ticks were dropped after they had been extracted, and they used to explode like popcorn.

There was one splendid incident. In the course of our training it was decided that we must prepare for the possibility of a gas attack. Gas masks were extremely primitive in those days and consisted of a hood rather like the Ku-Klux-Klan, made up of some evil-smelling material with enormous eye-pieces and nose-clips. On the appointed day we had to march on foot through a cloud of chlorine gas, first with our masks on and then with them off. I do not know which was the worse. Somebody then pointed out that it was not much use our surviving a gas attack if the camels did not, and it was decided to make an experiment. There happened to be available at the time a very sick camel, which had not eaten for days and was too weak to stand up. Very suitable for use as a guinea-pig. We all watched as the gas people projected a mass of their noxious compound at the unfortunate animal which disappeared completely for several minutes, at the end of which the cloud began to disperse and the camel was observed, to our great delight, to be standing on its feet for the first time for days and peacefully grazing! The chlorine had obviously met its match.

The barracks at Abbassia were old and primitive. The officers were billeted in what were alleged to be the married quarters and we had to contend with a variety of wild life, which included flies by day, mosquitoes by night, bugs at all times and some monstrous black hornets which had taken possession of our hut. They left us alone so long as we did not interfere with them but there was always a chance of some accidental contact and, as we were assured by the local experts that a single sting from one of these creatures was probably fatal and two certainly, it is not surprising that we kept as far away as possible.

After two months our initial training was supposedly complete and my company (No. 8) was ordered to proceed to a camp at a place called Shusha, near Samalut, which was about 150 miles south of Cairo, involving a march of several days, mostly along the west bank of the Nile. It would have been possible to send us by rail but it was felt that a protracted march like this, under reasonably civilised conditions, would be a good experience for us prior to embarking on any desert operations Shusha was one of the bases from which operations against the Senussi were being conducted in the general direction of the Baharia Oasis, which was one of their principal assembly areas, and a light railway was being built as a line of communication with our forward units.

The opening stages of the march from Abbassia were almost unbelievable. To start with we had to ride through the centre of Cairo, and in the second place this was the first occasion on which we had proceeded in full marching order complete with all our stores, provisions, cooking equipment, extra blankets, ammunition, Lewis guns and so forth, all of which had to be packed on spare camels, which had been specially selected to carry what were in fact enormous loads, not only in weight but size. Later on, of course, we got used to packing up all this paraphernalia almost in a matter of minutes and, more important still, packing it correctly so that the load was evenly spread, a vital necessity if saddle sores were to be avoided. But on this first occasion we had no experience of this sort of thing to draw on and it is not surprising that we made a very amateurish job of it, with the result that it was not very long before knots became untied, ropes began to loosen, loads started slipping and various pieces of equipment became detached and fell off.

Furthermore, we had not really learnt to control our camels properly and, what with the difficulty of guiding them through the Cairo traffic and continually having to dismount and pick up odds and ends of equipment which had fallen off the pack camels and struggling to reload them, it was not surprising that before long the column began to split up into little detached groups of camels, spread over a couple of miles or so with hardly any vestige of order or discipline left. On top of all this there were a number of stragglers to be rounded up and guided through the maze of streets which had to be negotiated. No doubt it was a salutary experience but it was also a painfully humiliating one and must have been a source of great amusement to the Egyptian population, who disliked us anyway and were always at pains to show us how much they resented our presence.

Our route to Samalut and Shusha led through a series of quite large towns, such as Wasta and Beni Suef, and for practically the whole way followed the bank of the river. The heat was terrific and we made a practice of starting off the day's march at about 4 a.m. and continuing for some four hours. We would then rest up during the heat of the day and start off another three-hour trek about 4 p.m.

It was really rather enjoyable, particularly the early morning ride, when it was relatively cool, and all the time we were gaining experience in looking after, managing and packing the camels.

In addition to the towns, we passed through numberless villages surrounded by palm groves and waterholes, which were usually occupied by the enormous water buffaloes used by the fellaheen, as the peasant population is called, for various tasks. These animals could be a bit tricky at times and on one occasion a particularly ferocious-looking specimen chased my batman, who was probably out on a scrounging expedition of some kind, about a quarter of a mile into camp. Everywhere the local population turned out to greet us, though I do not suppose they had the remotest idea who or what we were, and it was rather pleasant to be welcomed with smiling faces in place of the stares and scowls we usually encountered in Cairo. We particularly envied the children who seemed to spend most of their time bathing in the Nile, a refreshment which was denied us on account of that dreadful Egyptian disease bilharziosis. It seems that the waters of the Nile are infected with some sort of parasite or organism which penetrates every orifice of the body, including even the pores of the skin, and then proceeds to eat one's insides away. Not surprisingly, therefore, it was a court-martial offence if one was caught bathing.

At Beni Suef we received an astonishing entertainment. We were greeted by a number of Notables, as they were called, who delivered an invitation to the officers from the Mudir, or Governor of the province, to lunch or rather feast with him at his private residence. This was, of course, an invitation which had to be accepted and in due course we presented ourselves at the gates. There were about a dozen people present including the Mudir's A.D.C., some Egyptian officers and various Notables and we all squatted on the floor, something which I have always found very difficult to do, being rather stiff jointed, round a low table where we proceeded to consume the biggest meal with which I have ever been confronted. There were ten courses, but no implements of any kind, and the *pièce de résistance* was a mountain of chicken and rice into which we each in turn plunged our hands and, after finishing what we had succeeded in gathering, licked our fingers, and plunged them in again!

What with the food and beer with which we washed it down and the steadily increasing heat, both from within and without, we were dripping with sweat and almost beginning to lose consciousness when the Mudir announced that it was time for siesta. The fact that there was nothing on which to lie caused him no problem, and he charged out of the room clapping his hands and yelling directions at the top of his voice. We then became aware of a sort of twittering and giggling from the floor above, and caught an occasional glimpse of a dark-robed figure with a white veil which obscured the whole face apart from the eyes peering down on us. This was followed by a procession of servants down the stairs, each of them carrying a mattress which had unmistakably been filched from the Mudir's harem. The mattresses were laid side by side on the floor and we were invited to compose ourselves to rest. Not only was this another invitation which it would have been very impolite and indeed insulting to refuse, but by then we were in such a state of extremity that we would have been quite incapable of refusing anyway.

Never shall I forget the overpowering scent of patchouli which accompanied me as I lost consciousness and remained with me throughout my dreams.

Chapter Four

THE DESERT—BAHARIA—FAYOUM

A DAY or two later we reached Shusha camp, which was located just on the edge of the desert a mile or two from Samalut. I cannot recollect how many troops it contained or of what they consisted apart from the Royal Bucks Hussars, to whom we were attached for rations, etc., and whose commanding officer, Colonel John Grenfell, was the senior officer in the camp. Their adjutant was 'Tony' Rothschild, and I can remember messing with a squadron whose officers included Major ' Freddie ' Cripps, Neil Primrose, Lord Rosebery's son, and Evelyn Rothschild, both of whom were killed in Palestine a year or so later.

The building of the light railway was proceeding apace and now stretched about sixty miles into the desert. Four block-houses, which were located at intervals of about fifteen miles, had already been built B.1, B.2, B.3, and B.4, and two more were in process of construction.

After we had been at Shusha for two or three weeks it was decided to send a detachment of the Camel Corps to B.4, which was the forward base and Paterson and I, with our respective sections of Westminster Dragoons and Berkshire Yeomanry, were ordered to accompany it. It was our first training exercise on any sort of an operational basis and it was quite an exciting prospect.

I should explain here the enormous difficulty of mounting any operations against the Senussi in the Western desert. They were based on various oases far away in the interior, but there was no possible means of finding out where they were in strength at any particular time. It was believed that some 2000 tribesmen were gathered at Baharia which was our objective, but nobody seemed to know exactly where Baharia was. Such maps as existed were virtually useless and there were thousands of square miles of desert which appeared on them, either as a completely blank space or just with the one word ' unexplored '. There was no doubt that they were ' desert ' but the desert varied considerably. Some parts were soft sand, others hard gravel on both of which, particularly the latter, we could make good progress, but it was known that somewhere between us and Baharia there was a vast range of sand dunes more than a 100 miles long, anything up to eight miles wide and in places quite impenetrable. Somehow or other a way through had to be found if we were ever to reach the oasis which was believed to be about fifteen miles on from where the dunes died out.

This was my first experience of the real desert and I found that, despite or perhaps because of its utter silence and loneliness, it had an extraordinary fascination for me. Apart from our little party there was hardly a living creature to be seen. Occasionally one would glimpse the trail of a gazelle or the track of a lizard in the sand, but it was always a mystery to me how they survived, particularly the gazelle. There was no water and hardly any growth except for camel thorn which by some miracle of nature contained an element of moisture. Nor were there any birds to be seen and even insects were rare though occasionally one came across a praying mantis. One night I shared my sleeping bag with a scorpion which was not discovered till the morning. Fortunately we had slept in different compartments. There was also a ferocious species of spider, and at Shusha we used to put on spider fights which invariably ended in the death of one of the combatants and its consumption by the victor. Some of them became champions and I remember that our representative, which was known as 'The Shusha Slosher', had a great reputation throughout the camp, until it succumbed in its turn to a younger and stronger opponent.

It was now midsummer and during the daytime the desert was like a furnace. Violent dust storms blew up from nowhere without any warning and subsided just as quickly perhaps an hour later, by which time one's mouth and ears and nostrils were choked with sand and one's skin, wherever it was exposed, scorched and scarified. But it was not long before our knees and faces, which had started off by assuming a brilliant scarlet colour, became almost black and tough enough to stand up to almost anything in the way of heat which the desert could throw at us. Fortunately the nights were cool and sometimes cold, and we were able to get some sleep which was almost impossible when we were resting during the day. Water, of course, was the great problem, although not so acute at this stage when we were only cut off from fresh supplies for a day or two at a time. Later on when we were on patrol for four or even five consecutive days it was a constant anxiety. All we had for drinking and washing was a goatskin bottle and a five-gallon tank fixed to the saddle. Owing to the intense evaporation the water in the bottle remained refreshingly cool whatever the conditions, but unfortunately it also diminished the supply and we had to be careful not to run out. I remember this occurring on two occasions and it is not a very pleasant experience being without water in the desert even for a few hours especially, as happened once later on, when you are under shell fire.

Our progress to B.4 was relatively uneventful. We trekked during the cooler parts of the day and bedded down at night either in the desert or at one of the intermediate blockhouses. A good deal of patrolling was going on in every direction and, apart from the Camel Corps, this was usually carried out by detachments of armoured cars. These were known as the heavy and light patrols, and it is curious to reflect that although this was more than fifty years ago the former consisted of Rolls-Royces and the latter of Fords. There were no tracked vehicles in those days, and it was astonishing how these two makes of car were able to cope with virtually any kind of desert, sometimes covering more than 100 miles in a day. I do not mean that they could ride the dunes, this was of course impossible, but they could range far and wide until they found a gap through which to penetrate and, although this generally came to a dead end, they were able to make an occasional break-through and more or less plot the course which would have to be taken by the main body when the time came, months later, for the advance on Baharia. The dunes were certainly a fearful obstacle but it was not until my second tour of duty when I was stationed at B.6, which had been completed by then and become a railhead, that I came to grips with them for the first time.

Meanwhile there was a lot of patrolling to be done from B.4 but the furthest we could go fell far short of the dunes themselves. After we had been there for a few days I was ordered to take a patrol with half a dozen men and penetrate as far as we could into the broken ground which stretched for miles between the blockhouse and the dunes and ascertain whether any sort of Senussi activity was going on. This ' broken ground ' was a deadly sort of place. The going was quite good but, owing to the endless number of mounds and hillocks, some of them as much as 200 feet high, it was impossible to see for any distance in any direction or to keep a straight course and, as we found, it was very easy to get lost.

There had been a caravan route of some kind but we were never able to discover where it led from and, worse still, where it was going, in addition to which the tracks were constantly diverging and breaking away from each other. There was no indication whether it had been used in recent weeks or months or even years and it was really no use to us at all. Each hillock had a completely flat top, and frequently this was surmounted by a cairn of stones, but we had no idea what they signified. There was no water, no growth and no sign of life, nothing but sand, gravel, rock and during the daytime a burning shimmering heat which distorted everything into fantastic shapes and images. Things were not made any easier by the fact that we were supposedly in enemy territory and had received orders to be always on the strictest guard and never to show ourselves on any skyline and I must admit that, as our trusty camels bore us further into this dreadful wilderness, we began to feel very small and lonely. Our way did not lead straight as we were continually having to circumvent hillocks of various sizes and although, of course, I could with the help of my compass (not 100 per cent reliable among those rocks), the sun by day and the stars by night more or less determine the direction in which we were going, I could not forget that B.4 was nothing but a pin point which it would be very easy to miss on the return journey and that our water would not stretch in those conditions beyond four days at the most.

In due course we began the return journey. There was, of course, no problem as regards direction. All we had to do was to proceed due east. The difficulty would arise when we emerged into the flat desert when I should have to decide whether we were north or south of B.4 or in a direct line. Otherwise it would be only too easy to miss it, and our water was already running short. In fact it ran out altogether during the evening of the third day since leaving B.4 which was when we finally broke through with still another fifteen or twenty miles to go before we reached the blockhouse, always assuming that we were going in the right direction. I decided to wait until morning before we moved on, and we had the prospect of a very anxious and thirsty night ahead of us. And then, to our intense relief, two tiny specks appeared on the horizon which soon resolved themselves into a couple of Rolls-Royce armoured cars which had been sent out to try and locate us. They had a little water with them, but not quite sufficient for our needs, and eventually the water was drained from the radiator of one of the cars which, of course, immobilised it, leaving the other to return to base in the morning and come back with fresh supplies. So it all ended very happily and I was very glad that I had not been called upon to make the final decision.

By this ,time our company commander Captain Mason-MacFarlane, a brilliant regular officer who had come to us from the 7th Hussars, had arrived from Shusha, and after a few days it was decided that I and my section should be relieved and return to Shusha, to be replaced by an officer called Ryan with his section from the Dorset Yeomanry. In due course Ryan and his men arrived and we marched out the next day on our trek back to base. I had expected to stay at Shusha for some time but I had only been there a few days when I was ordered to proceed with about thirty men to the Fayoum Oasis, which was about sixty miles to the north. The Fayoum is really more than an oasis and covers a wide area of very fertile country separated from the Nile Valley by a strip of desert which in places is only about a mile wide. We were to be attached to the Lincolnshire Yeomanry who were camped on the southern fringe of the oasis. More about that later, but first of all I must relate the story of MacFarlane and Ryan.

MacFarlane was a man of great energy, resource and courage and it was not long before he decided to make a personal reconnaissance of the Baharia itself, provided that a way could be found through the dunes for a patrol mounted on the best and hardiest camels available. At best this was going to be a very hazardous and dangerous mission, but just possible within the limit of five days. It was believed, and so it turned out, that the oasis lay in a deep depression surrounded by a high escarpment and it would, of course, be necessary to remain on the high ground until the patrol could proceed to the lower level under cover of darkness. Eventually, with the help of the armoured cars, a viable route through the dunes was found and a day fixed for the operation to start. On this occasion MacFarlane was accompanied by Paterson and a Sergeant Guppy from the Dorset Yeomanry section. Everything proceeded according to plan, all MacFarlane's calculations turned out to be correct, and on a late afternoon the patrol established itself on top of the cliff from where they could not only see the oasis spread out below them but also observe that a little distance away it could be approached through a gap in the escarpment, which would provide them with a relatively easy access to the lower ground.

Directly it was dark enough they started off and rode down the slope to a point a few hundred yards away from the fringe of the oasis, where they halted and dismounted. MacFarlane then proceeded to carry out a personal reconnaissance on foot which took him right through the oasis to the other side and back, a distance of some nine or ten miles on a moonless night through country which he had never seen and was quite un-mapped, and which was infested with a merciless enemy. His orders to Paterson and Guppy were that, if he had not returned by dawn, they were not to wait for him any longer and in fact it was obvious that with the arrival of daylight they would have no chance of survival. The night wore on and the false dawn had already come and gone when they heard the footsteps of a running man and MacFarlane emerged from the darkness which was already lightening. He was speechless from exhaustion and thirst, but indicated that there was no time to lose, and within seconds they were on their camels and away. At the same time figures could dimly be seen rushing out of the oasis, there was a fusillade of rifle fire but nobody was hit and, before the Arabs could organise any sort of pursuit, the patrol was racing up the slope to the escarpment and going flat out back towards the dunes and safety. Not the least incredible part of this feat of valour and endurance was that on his return MacFarlane was able to reproduce a rough map of the Baharia which turned out to be substantially accurate and this despite the fact that, from the moment he entered the oasis until he left it, he was aware of being shadowed from behind and both sides, and he was quite unable to understand why his pursuers had not closed in on him until it was just too late.

Some two or three weeks later MacFarlane decided to make another reconnaissance to complete his study of the oasis and to form some idea of the strength in which it was held. It was believed that there were at least 2000 Senussi in the area. On this occasion he was accompanied by Ryan, a Corporal Bolt and two other Dorset men and they made their landfall at the top of the escarpment sometime in the late afternoon of the second day. It seems that MacFarlane decided that he and Ryan should proceed on foot some way along the top of the cliff to a point where they could get a better view of the oasis. Bolt was ordered to keep all five camels ready saddled for a quick getaway in the event of an emergency, but was told that in any case the two officers would be back within the hour. About an hour later Bolt's little party heard the sound of heavy firing some distance away in the direction in which they had gone. After a minute or two there was silence, but there was no sign of the officers returning and Bolt was faced with the heavy responsibility of deciding what he should do. And then suddenly he became aware that a large party of tribesmen were climbing up the cliff towards him and that, whatever had happened to the officers, he had now got a fight on his own hands.

There ensued a battle which was quite a little epic in its way. From where they lay on the top of the cliff they opened fire on the tribesmen, who were by then only thrity feet below and, besides inflicting several casualties, they were able to pin the remainder of the party down. However, with the approach of darkness it was obvious that, if they stayed there, it would only be a matter of time before they were overwhelmed. Furthermore there was still no sign of MacFarlane and Ryan, and it could only be concluded that they had come to some harm. The only choice seemed to be retreat, but it was very difficult to disengage without being rushed by the enemy, and Bolt decided to put up a bluff. He ordered the other two to take all the camels back a few hundred yards and he would join them as soon as he could. He then took on the enemy single-handed, changing his position every few seconds and firing from a different point so as to give the impression that the party was still intact. Fortunately the tribesmen seemed reluctant to come out in the open and rush those last thirty feet. After a final burst of fire Bolt ran literally for his life back to the camels and as the tribesmen appeared over the top of the cliff they were on their way. Two days later the forlorn little party of three exhausted men and five camels arrived back at B.4 and Bolt put in his report.

But, of course, he was in the unhappy position of having returned from a dangerous patrol without his officers and the question arose as to whether his story could be accepted out of hand or whether there should be a court of enquiry or even a court martial. And then, while this was being decided by higher authority, he had a lucky break. A Bedouin was picked up by a patrol and it turned out that he had been a witness of the whole affair. Not only did he corroborate Bolt's account but he was able to tell what had happened to MacFarlane and Ryan. It seems that they had been attacked in the same way as the others but they had not been able to prevent the tribesmen scaling the cliff. There had been a grim battle at a few yards' range between the two officers, armed only with revolvers, and dozens of tribesmen armed with rifles. Several of the latter were killed but, of course, the outcome was inevitable. The Bedouin believed that one of the revolvers jammed and the other ran out of ammunition, and all that MacFarlane and Ryan could do was to throw first of all their revolvers and then stones at the enemy until after a few seconds they were shot down,

I.C.C.—4

and their bodies flung over the cliff, where they were found when the oasis was taken a couple of months later. So instead of a court martial Bolt was recommened for a V.C. as a reward for his outstanding courage and resource but, incomprehensibly, all he received was an Italian decoration, Italy having just come into the war. However, he made up for this later in the war by getting the D.C.M. and Bar. It was widely believed that MacFarlane was also put up for a posthumous V.C., an honour which we all thought he richly deserved.

I heard the news when I was in the Fayoum, where I spent several weeks carrying out various patrol duties. I remember one of these patrols particularly well. For some reason which was a little obscure at the time, and is even more so now, I was ordered to take with me a local Sheikh. Nobody seemed to know whether he was going to disclose to us the whereabouts of a band of Senussi or whether he was likely to lead us into a trap or whether he was simply attached as a guide. All I can remember about him is that he was a giant of a man and suffering badly from bilharziosis. Neither of us could understand a single word the other said and we took an intense dislike to each other on sight.

It was a very small patrol and my orders were about as vague as they could be apart from the fact that we were to be out in the desert for four days and ascertain whether there was any sign of the elusive Senussi. Late one afternoon we arrived at a range of high dunes and I decided to camp for the night. But we had no sooner dismounted when the Sheikh suddenly took to his heels and bolted through a gap in the nearest dune. I shouted to him to stop but this had no effect and the only thing I could do was to follow him. By then I was convinced that he was going to sell us down the river, not a very apt metaphor in that sandy wilderness, and I thought I might have to shoot him. It was a nightmare chase up and down the dunes, stumbling about in the loose drifting sand, cursing and swearing

at each other, sweating like bulls (at least I was) in the blazing
heat until finally with a last savage imprecation the old boy
squatted down and proceeded to relieve himself. As I have
said, he was suffering from bilharziosis and he appeared to be
undergoing a particularly acute attack. All the poor man was
looking for was a little privacy, and our arrival at the dunes
had given him the opportunity. I turned my back and a little
later he rose and we walked back to camp without a word.

We had another patrol a few days later which had a tragic
instead of a comic sequel. One of the men was a veterinary
corporal whose job it was to attend to the various ailments
which afflicted our hard-worked camels. I suppose that his
continual contact with the different kinds of septicaemia from
which they suffered had infected him, and I remember that
he had a number of bandages on the exposed surfaces of his
body such as knees, arms, neck, etc. This did not call for any
particular comment as most of us were suffering from sores of
one kind or another, and indeed this was general throughout the
whole of the army in Egypt. The same thing happened, I
believe, to the troops in South Africa during the Boer War
where they were called 'veldt' sores. They were due to a
variety of causes, such as lack of fresh vegetables, infected water,
and bites from various mosquitoes and sand-flies, to say nothing
of ordinary flies which pestered us in thousands from morning
to night. Even when we went into the desert we always took
hundreds of these loathsome little creatures with us on ourselves
and our camels, and on long expeditions it was several days
before they died out. On shorter ones we simply brought them
back with us. I think that everyone was infected in some degree.
Even if you simply cut yourself shaving the chances were that it
would turn septic and some of the men had sores all over their
faces. I had a few myself and they were very difficult to cure
because of the bristles growing through the open sores.

Anyway, when we were about two days out on patrol, the

corporal was taken desperately ill. I will not attempt to describe
what the unfortunate man had to go through but, mercifully,
after a few hours he relapsed into unconsciousness, and we
certainly had a problem on our hands. I sent two men back to
camp for help and we did our best for the patient until it arrived.
After all this time I cannot remember the details but an ambulance
of some kind was sent out and he was taken on ahead. After
we got back ourselves I was met by the medical officer in charge,
who was a very worried man, and he asked me to come with
him and see the patient, who had been put into a separate hut.
He was still unconscious but while we were with him he went
into a terrible convulsion and died. The M.O. told me that he
suspected cholera and was sending in a report to that effect.
Supplies of vaccine were rushed into the camp and, pending an
autopsy, everybody had to be inoculated. The autopsy took
place two days later in the town of Fayoum, but it was not until
after several days that we heard that the death had not been caused
by cholera, but by some other virus which the medical people had
been quite unable to identify. Fortunately it cannot have been
contagious or infectious as nobody else succumbed, but they
were very anxious days and I cannot say that the detachment
from the Camel Corps was exactly popular until the flap
eventually died down.

But there were so many diseases about including dysentery,
malaria, sand-fly fever, etc., and there was always the danger of
typhoid although, of course, we had all been inoculated against
this either before we left England or on the ship. There was
also an outbreak of plague throughout the Fayoum Oasis, where
it was probably more or less endemic, and there were several
villages which we were not allowed to pass through, even in a
car, without taking precautions. We had to stop a few hundred
yards short of the village and cover our faces with a sort of
gauze mask before driving through hell-for-leather, with orders
not to stop under any circumstances whatever, not even if we

killed or injured one of the inhabitants. So far as I know there was no accident of this kind but on the one or two occasions when I had to drive, or rather be driven, through one of the villages we always left a trail of dead or injured dogs, chickens, sheep, goats and so forth behind us. I cannot think that this endeared us particularly to the unfortunate villagers, who already had the plague to contend with, but it would have been disastrous if on top of all its other troubles the army had become plague ridden.

After about two months we took leave of the Lincolnshire Yeomanry and returned to Shusha, where the final capture of the Baharia was being planned. B.6 had now been completed and become railhead which, of course, enormously eased the problem of supplies. The company had been taken over by Paterson, who before the war had been in China with the well-known merchant firm of Jardine Matheson & Company, and returned there when the war was over. In the Second War he was in command of the Hong Kong Home Guard, which put up a terrific resistance against the Japanese until, having run out of food and ammunition, it was forced to surrender after being completely encircled and sustaining heavy casualties.

In point of fact there is little to relate about the operations against the Baharia because the Senussi had seen the writing on the wall and decided to get out while the going was good. The advance took place in October and November, 1916, and it was interesting to pass once more over the ground which we had patrolled earlier in the year, make our way at last through the range of sand dunes to the open ground beyond and then for about fifteen miles to the escarpment surrounding the oasis where MacFarlane and Ryan had died, and down through the gap between the cliffs to the verge of the oasis itself, which would have looked and seemed peaceful enough had it not been for their bodies, which were found lying at the bottom of the cliff.

My chief recollection of the Baharia is that it was a very beautiful place with a profusion of date palms, groves of oranges and limes and virtually unlimited water and marshland, which abounded with duck of various species, snipe and other water-fowl. A less attractive feature was the fact that most of the Arab children were afflicted with elephantiasis and in many cases their heads were at least twice the normal size, which gave them a grotesque appearance. In the absence of the Senussi fighting men the inhabitants received us peacefully enough and supplied our wants of fresh fruit and vegetables, which were very welcome after months of bully beef and biscuit and other army rations which though quite good of their kind were distinctly monotonous.

But the highlight was a truly memorable feast. One of my colleagues borrowed a gun from somewhere and shot several duck and teal which we cooked ourselves over a very low fire in the largest pot we could lay our hands on and to which we added a magnificent sauce composed of tinned cream, a pound or two of crystallised plums and a whole bottle of port, which we had carried for hundreds of miles waiting for a real occasion to arise. This was the occasion. The sauce was almost black, with the consistency of the thickest lentil soup, and we took turns to pour it with loving hands over those marvellous birds. The preparation of the meal took hours and the smell from that fragrant concoction had made us almost demented by the time it was ready to eat. But it was worth waiting for and I have never in my life tasted anything so delicious.

In the meantime reports had been coming in from Jennings Bramley's Intelligence that the Senussi had withdrawn to the oasis of Farafra, 120 miles further to the south. It was not known whether they intended to make a stand there but this was something which had to be discovered and a force of fifty men was dispatched for this purpose under the command of Jennings Bramley himself, who had been in Egypt for thirty years and held the rank of Bimbashi (Colonel) in the Egyptian army.

It was realised that, if any serious resistance was encountered and they were unable to get into the oasis, they would be faced with the prospect of having to get back without any chance of replenishing their water supplies, a march of 240 miles which would take at least six days to accomplish, and would be a very severe ordeal for men and camels alike. However, in the result, all was well as most of the Senussi had already melted away into the desert and the party returned safely to the Baharia with fifteen prisoners. Mr Mark Ward of Weymouth has given an account of this expedition, in which he took part with a number of other men from No. 8 Company, and he also recalls, something which I do not myself recollect, that some of the patrols which penetrated the great mass of sand dunes which stood between the Baharia and B.6, which was the last of the block-houses, were considered to be so dangerous that knock-out pills were issued to be used in the event of capture, as there had been several cases of torture and mutilation on the part of the Senussi. Something of this sort had been witnessed by John Ressich as he lay unable to move at the bottom of the wadi after the disastrous charge which I have already related. On another occasion a Yeomanry officer, whose name I will not divulge, though I knew him well, was so incensed when he came across a party of three or four Senussi horribly mutilating the body of a British soldier that, although normally the gentlest of men, he lined them up in a row and shot them one by one at point blank range with his revolver. The danger of falling into the hands of the Senussi was well known to everybody, which throws into sharp relief the reply which was given by a very senior officer to a question as to whether there was any news of Mason-MacFarlane and Ryan—' Not so far ' he said ' But they will be all right. The Senussi are gentlemen and will treat them decently.' Well perhaps they would have, but it may have been fortunate for those two brave men that, as it turned out, they were killed on the spot fighting to the last round in their revolvers.

We did not stay in the Baharia for more than a few days before returning to B.6 where my section of the Berkshire Yeomanry and the section of the Royal Bucks Hussars commanded by a friend of mine, Merlin Huth, were attached to the Montgomeryshire Yeomanry who occupied the post and one of whose officers was the present Mr Justice Stable. The rest of the company proceeded to Shusha where we rejoined them towards the end of January, 1917.

Before we left B.6 Huth and I made two interesting discoveries. Walking along the edge of the dunes one evening we came across a vast area of oyster shells which, although we were anything between 500 and 1000 feet above sea-level, afforded pretty convincing proof that at some remote time in the past the whole of this part of the desert was under the sea. The other discovery was that camels can eat anything. At any rate one of them on which we experimented one day consumed, apparently to its complete satisfaction and without any ill effects whatever, two or three tins of salmon, tins and all, and several boxes of matches This may sound rather cruel but we had the feeling, based on previous experience, that a camel's digestive processes were capable of absorbing anything he was offered, and how right we were!

Shortly after our return to Shusha the company was ordered to return to its old quarters at Abbassia. The journey was to be made by rail and we made another discovery, which is that camels have a rooted objection to getting into trains. There were ramps leading up to the camel trucks and all the pushing and pulling and swearing in the world would not induce the camels to climb them. However, somebody produced a very bright idea. We wrapped their heads in an assortment of sacks and blankets, turned them round several times so as to get them

confused as to direction, manoeuvred their backsides towards
the ramps and then pulled for all we were worth in the opposite
direction. This was quite sufficient to induce the camels to go
backwards up the ramps, and in next to no time we had the
whole lot safely entrained and tethered down. Their astonish-
ment and disgust when their head covering was removed were
almost pathetic. For once they had been fooled into doing
what we wanted and they obviously regarded the whole thing
as a very shabby trick.

Chapter Five

THE SOUTHERN OASES

If AN imaginary line is drawn due south from Sollum on the coast to the Siwa Oasis and from there south east and south to the oases of Baharia, Farafra, Dahkla and Kharga the territory enclosed between that line to the west, the sea to the north and the Nile Valley to the east comprises an area of more than 50,000 square miles, considerable parts of which had to be constantly patrolled after the withdrawal of the main body of the Senussi from the coastal regions into the interior of the Western Desert, and this was precisely the task for which the Imperial Camel Corps had originally been formed.

At about the same time that we had left Abbassia for our Baharian adventures the other companies were either sent direct to Sinai to join up with the forces covering the Suez Canal or to various places within the Kharga area to strengthen or replace the cavalry and for that matter infantry units which were already there but, with the approach of summer, were becoming more and more unsuited to the task which lay ahead.

The Kharga expedition included No. 10 Company and to reach the oasis, which lies about 250 miles to the south east of Baharia, they had to proceed by rail from Cairo to the nearest station and from there undertake a march of 100 miles across the intervening desert.

Kharga is a large and well watered oasis with several villages and noted particularly for its fine dates. About 100 miles to the west there is the oasis of Dahkla and, when the Senussi were being driven into the interior from the coastal regions, they were reported to be concentrating at Dahkla as well as Baharia, which was the reason for the decision that Kharga should be occupied so as to keep an eye on their movements. Part of a Scottish Infantry brigade had been sent to this area but the occupation of the outlying posts and the whole of the patrolling in the general direction of Dahkla were made the responsibility of the Camel Corps. Wing Commander Ashlin, who was then a Lieutenant in No. 10 Company, was in charge of the furthermost post which consisted of a stone building surrounded by a wall and was turned into some semblance of a fort   It covered the principal approach to Kharga from the desert and all the long distance patrols operated from this point. Ashlin's command included a platoon of a Highland regiment and he had given orders that no pipes were to play within a quarter of a mile of the camel lines, because the first time the camels heard the pipes there was a stampede and it took several hours to round them up. After this incident the relations between the Scotties and the camels became severely strained and they never succeeded in getting over their mutual distrust and dislike. To the Scotties a camel was always a ' bluidy hump ' and it would be interesting to know exactly what the camels thought in return!

Ashlin has given a graphic account of one of the patrols which he led towards the Dahkla Oasis. It was an exceptionally unpleasant one but the story does help to illustrate the dangers and discomforts of operating in those barren and waterless wastes, which were for the most part unmapped and even unexplored. In addition it was now mid-summer and the desert was like a furnace. Kharga Oasis is in a hollow and to get out of it, in the only direction patrols could go towards Dahkla, it was necessary to cover about forty-five miles of flat desert, dotted here and there with a well or waterhole, and then climb an almost perpendicular escarpment between 300 and

400 feet high. There was only one steep path, within a radius of 100 miles in the required direction, leading up to the top of the plateau, and it was particularly hard to find, so much so that, as this was to be their first long patrol, Ashlin took with him as guides two Australians who had been there before with their own company of Imperial Camel Corps and were supposed to know the path well.

I now propose to give the story of what happened in Ashlin's own words which, although I was to have my own fair share of patrolling in the Baharia and other sectors, are far more descriptive and indeed exciting than any I could use at second hand.

This patrol was a particularly long one (seven days). We were supposed to strike some wells reported to be at a certain point on our way. The patrol consisted of eleven all told including the two guides and myself. Fortunately I had picked out my animals carefully and brought four spares. Nothing untoward happened until we got to the reported wells which we found to be bone dry. There was a little camel scrub close by which refreshed the animals to some extent and, although we had not been economising particularly with our drinking water, we still had sufficient, with careful rationing, for three days which would just get us back. One of the first lessons taught in the Imperial Camel Corps was to husband one's water supply on such expeditions, and consequently there was no cause for alarm. The going had been heavy, men and animals were tired and a *Khamseen* (sand storm) was blowing, so we camped for a few hours and tried to get what rest we could with our heads buried in our blankets. The rest refreshed the animals, though it did us little good, and we made good time going back, reaching the edge of the escarpment on the morning of the sixth day without water for the camels. We could see far below us at a distance of thirty miles the dark outline of a small oasis indicating the location of water. All that remained was to find the path down and in five or six hours we would be drinking our fill. Both our guides seemed quite certain that we had struck the edge of the escarpment to the north of the path, so we turned south. The *Khamseen*, as happens so often in those parts, had completely changed the aspect of the country owing to the shifting sand, so there was some excuse for the guides' mistake. This, however, should not have happened if we had been more experienced.

At the end of three hours' marching there was still no trace of the opening in the escarpment. The camels were showing signs of distress and we began to realise the predicament we were in. The guides were now frankly at a loss, so after a short halt I decided to retrace our steps. It was noon with the heat at its highest but I dared not halt for more than a breather. Naturally our progress was very much slower and it was almost night when we reached the point where we first struck the edge of the escarpment. Darkness was fast falling so there was nothing to do but camp. The animals were suffering acutely and our drinking water was practically all gone. I collected what was left and it did not fill one small water bottle. We spent an anxious night. It was too dark to try and locate the path so we had to wait with what patience we could for the coming of dawn. As soon as it was light enough we started, our progress being now painfully slow as we had to halt frequently and lead the camels over the worst bits of ground.

We had been plodding along for about two hours when one of the weaker animals went mad with thirst. The poor beast was too weak to do any damage and, as it was in agony, we shot it. Shortly after another, fortunately a spare which had gone lame, also went mad and fell over the escarpment. He must have broken his neck because he lay still at the bottom. Towards noon after covering about fifteen miles without finding the path, our worst misfortune overtook us. One of the Australian guides, quite a young boy, began to behave queerly, from thirst, the sun or probably both. He became delirious and so violent that we had to bind him to his saddle. I then decided to give up looking for the path, realising that our only course was to make an attempt to descend the escarpment. This was no task at all for us on foot. The difficulty was to get the camels down, it looked almost impossible without breaking their legs, particularly in their weakened condition. Without camels it was doubtful if we could have traversed those thirty miles of desert to the nearest well. Something had to be done, however, and I hoped with luck that two or three animals might reach the bottom uninjured and we could fetch water and help.

We found a place which resembled a very steep chute reaching to about forty feet from the bottom. It zigzagged a little and there was a certain amount of loose sand and stones on the surface. Half the men descended and we rolled the kit and equipment down. Then we tackled the chief problem which was getting the animals to descend, and it was then that they showed their intelligence and good sense. They seemed to know that it was their only chance. We coaxed the first one over the edge and into the chute. As soon as he felt himself going he just sat down on his haunches and slid which was the only possible way of getting down without a broken neck. We got the others down in the same way and in quick succession. The last forty feet was practically a sheer drop but they rolled or scrambled down somehow. They were all, of course, badly cut and scraped by the rocks and some were lamed but actually there were only two serious casualties, both broken legs. These animals had to be shot. Although we only lost four camels some were so weak and lame that they could not be ridden and the less exhausted carried a double burden on this last lap of our journey. It was with very thankful hearts that we made for the well which, owing to this episode, was named the Well of Deliverance and so marked in the survey maps. The camels seemed to sense that water was near for we covered the thirty miles in a little over six hours in spite of their exhausted condition. We subsequently discovered that the *Khamseen* had obliterated all signs of the path down the escarpment, and a land mark was put up so that there should be no repetition of this unpleasant incident.

I should just like to add that following a survey trek between Kharga and Dahkla this officer had a hill named after him— ' Mount Ashlin '.

At the end of July No. 10 Company proceeded to Sinai where it joined up with Nos. 6, 7 and 9 Companies and as part of the Desert Mobile Column became heavily engaged over the next two months in the Battle of Romani and subsequent operations as described in the following chapters. Towards the end of September it returned to Kharga which had been held during its absence in Sinai by a battalion of infantry, who naturally had been unable to maintain the long range desert patrols. Consequently remnants of the Senussi forces had managed to concentrate in the oasis of Dahkla about 100 miles to the west, in the same way as they had been able to occupy the oasis of Baharia 150 miles further to the north, and it was decided that the time had come for both of these places to be captured and the Senussi driven beyond the frontiers of Egypt. Dahkla had always been one of their strongholds although officially administered by the Egyptian Government.

On arrival back in Kharga No. 10 Company immediately resumed its patrolling towards the fringes of Dahkla. These were helped by a water and ration dump which had been established thirty miles to the west of Kharga, apart from which the five-day patrols were over entirely waterless desert. The patrols had now been increased in strength and early in October a small force of about two sections, comprising some sixty rifles and two Lewis guns, encountered a group of Senussi a few miles to the east of the first well in the Dahkla Oasis. The Camel Corps were a good deal more mobile than the Arabs who were soon rounded up. They were mostly on foot although they had with them a few scrawny female camels, each bearing the Senussi brand or *wasm* which is a tribal brand as distinct from a *fendy* which denotes a sub-clan. Incidentally each camel of the Imperial Camel Corps had its own regimental number which was branded on its neck. This particular party of Senussi was made up from several sub-clans, but as all their camels bore the regular Senussi *wasm*, a shortened version of the Arabic word ' Allah ', they probably came from the ' Zawia ' or Monastery in Dahkla.

There was no other course than to escort all the prisoners back to Kharga, nearly ninety miles away and, as they were on foot, the Camel Corps were unable to ride at the usual short trot of six miles an hour and the whole column had to proceed at a slow walk. At one of the mid-day halts there was a sudden commotion among the Arab women, who had insisted on accompanying their menfolk into captivity, but it was not until it cried out that the Camel Corps realised that one of the women had given birth to a baby. It was explained to the Senussi leader that in two hours time the march would have to be resumed but a spare camel would be provided for the mother and child. This offer was, however, contemptuously refused presumably in order to prove that Senussi women were really tough and sure enough, as the column moved off, the woman was seen to make a sling of her rags, pop the baby in and fling it over her shoulder. And barefoot she made the march which had several more days to go.

Some of the men were clad in tatters of khaki uniform but most wore normal Bedouin clothing. Their arms consisted in the main of German Mausers or Russian rifles, but some of them carried the long Arab Jezel, a smooth bore flintlock about five feet long and usually decorated with mother of pearl inlaid in the butt and the barrel banded with silver. This weapon had a very short range, not more than 200 yards, and fired a home-moulded leaden bullet which could tear a nasty hole if it hit its mark. Most of the prisoners claimed to have come from the oasis of Jaghabub or the Jebel Akhdar, both of them hundreds of miles away to the north west in Cyrenaica.

There were several different routes between Kharga and Dahkla all of which had to be constantly patrolled. The desert in this region was exceptionally bare and there was no vegetation for the camels to graze, not even the seemingly dried up camel thorn, which would also have provided fuel for the cooking fires.

In the middle of October, at the same time as No. 8 Company was feeling its way towards the Baharia Oasis, it was decided that No. 10 Company should make an attempt to occupy Dahkla. Major T. Bardwell who had brought it down from Sinai had just taken up an appointment in the Sudan and the Company was commanded by Captain A. G. Wilkinson.

Pending its departure from Kharga it was attached to a Base Camp ' for pay and rations '. Not that pay was of much interest in the desert apart from a little mild gambling, but there was a Y.M.C.A. hut in the Camp, where it was possible to buy a few little luxuries to augment the perpetual bully beef and biscuits. The Camp was a large one and surrounded by barbed wire and piles of sandbags, with sentries perched on towers and protected from the sun by wooden canopies.

The Camp Commandant may have considered that the Camel Corps had its uses but he refused to have the camels within the perimeter of the barbed wire, even though there was plenty of room and, of course, the cameliers stayed with them   After all they had become quite used to sleeping in each others company! Normal rations were issued but no firewood, a situation which obviously had to be rectified. Following their last evening in the Camp canteen the cameliers were ordered outside the wire and the gates closed behind them but, unfortunately for the Commandant, he had not allowed for their skill and experience as night raiders. During the night not a single sentry gave the alarm and not a sound was heard except the usual croaking of the bull-frogs, the ticking of crickets and the light tapping of some sort of night bird, accompanied by the howling of jackals and the occasional moaning or bubbling of the camels.

Next morning the Company was saddled up in full ' Marching Order ' to move off when the Commandant rode out not to wave farewell but to complain that marauders had almost wrecked his camp. Whole wooden ablution benches and latrine screens (both of which the cameliers regarded with con-tempt!) had disappeared together with his favourite jackal trap and he wanted to know whether the Camel Corps were respons-ible. Not surprisingly he got very little change out of that and, although he walked right through the lines of camels peering and prying about in all directions, not a piece of his precious timber was to be seen. It had all been shredded by bayonets into sticks of about eighteen inches and tucked out of sight under the saddle bags and covering *furwahs* or blankets. I do not think that the cameliers, or buccaneers as I have more than once heard them called, were ever lacking in enterprise!

As it happened Dahkla was eventually taken without a struggle. The Senussi had been given sufficient evidence of the strength and mobility of the Camel Corps during the earlier skirmish and fled as it approached Tenida, the first village, where Headquarters was established while patrols were pushed further into the chain of village oases until finally the most westerly, Qasr el Dahkla, was occupied.

In his account of this expedition Laurence Moore has explained that Dahkla Oasis is rather different from that of Kharga. The villages are closer together and, owing to a much better water supply, it is a good deal more fertile. Dates, various citrus fruits and olives were grown and chickens and eggs could be bought from the villagers. A great escarpment, about 350 feet high, runs east to west, protecting the thirty-mile chain of villages from the prevailing northerly winds. Beyond Qasr el Dahkla the escarpment takes a sudden turn almost at a northern right angle and in this angle the last outpost was established at Bir Sheikh Mohammed, where lovely hot springs ran into deep stone cisterns. Communications were by heliograph so that, in order to get the mirror signals round the bend in the escarpment, three or four men were continually manning a transmitting station up on the highest point at the turn. From Bir Sheikh Mohammed nightly patrols ascended a nearby pass up the cliff and longer ones took trips of several days to the west in track of the Senussi, who were reported to have retreated to the oasis of Kufra, later to be made famous by the woman explorer Rosita Forbes.

Rumours of an impending counter-attack by the Senussi ' Army ' were continually being received but it never materialised which was perhaps just as well bearing in mind that the whole of the oasis was more than 100 miles from the nearest base at Kharga (which in any case could not have provided any reinforcements without the use of camels) and held by one company of Imperial Camel Corps and that almost the whole of its population was either of the Senussi Sect or allied to its cause.

No. 10 Company remained in Dahkla until May, 1917, when it was sent to Sollum to relieve No. 8 Company, which had been ordered to proceed to Sinai.

Chapter Six

SINAI—ROMANI

BEFORE RELATING the experiences of the Imperial Camel Corps in Sinai during the latter half of 1916 it might be helpful if I were to go back a bit and give a very brief account of the military situation in July of that year and of the events which led up to it.

In February, 1915, the Turks had made an attempt to invade Egypt across the Sinai Peninsula. The probable reasons for this were (1) to ensure that as many British soldiers as possible were retained to garrison the country and correspondingly reduce the number of troops available for the fighting in France, which would in turn release some of the German troops to strengthen their forces on the Russian front, at that time under considerable pressure and (2) to obtain a Turkish victory, on the only front where this was even remotely possible at the time, so as to counter the unpopularity of the war as a whole in Turkey and the possibility of a revolution.

Unfortunately for the Turks their rather slow and cumbrous movements towards the Suez Canal had been under close observation for several weeks, both by British aerial reconnaissance and patrols of the Egyptian and Bikanir Camel Corps, with the result that by the time the advanced units of the Turkish army which consisted, with its rear echelons, of about 60,000 regular and 10,000 irregular troops under the command of Djemal Pasha with a mixed Turco-German staff, reached the Canal, Sir John Maxwell had succeeded in collecting together a force of more than 40,000 men in entrenched positions on its western bank, which had been carefully prepared and strenthened for months previously, with another 30,000 in reserve. These included British, Indian, Australian and New Zealand troops and a considerable part of the native Egyptian army.

The attack when it came at dawn on the 3rd February, was badly conceived and handled and, instead of pushing forward reconnoitring columns to probe the British positions and ascertain how strongly they were held, or alternatively striking with his whole force, the Turkish commander more or less blundered up against the defences with a relatively weak force of not more than two below strength divisions, which were bloodily repulsed, and he never succeeded in getting the main body of his army into action at all. The Turks fought gallantly as usual but to no avail and by nightfall they were in full retreat.

It was estimated that their losses were not less than 4000 officers and men killed, wounded and taken prisoner, while the British casualties barely totalled sixty. In addition the Turks had lost practically all the pontoons which they had brought up for their intended crossing of the Canal.

No attempt was made to follow the retreating enemy, which was a wise decision in view of the fact that the British troops were not positioned to take the offensive nor were they yet sufficiently trained to take part in a major desert campaign. However, during the following months, a system of military defences was established well to the east of the Canal, pipelines and light railway and motor tracks were laid, and everything possible was done to ensure that, when winter came and conditions had become less rigorous in the wilderness which faced them, the British forces would be so strongly placed that they would not only be able to block any further attack on the Canal but also to take the offensive directly the opportunity arose.

In the meantime the British attack on the Dardanelles and

landings in Gallipoli had relieved the pressure by the Turks on other fronts and, although a second attempt on the Canal had been expected and Djemal Pasha had asked for 25,000 German troops to reinforce his battered army, there was very little chance of his request being granted and, in the event, he had to wait some time for reinforcements from any source.

In consequence he refused to make any further move towards the Canal and by the end of 1915 the British were beginning to worry his advanced posts.

In February, 1916, the great German reservoir at Hassana, 100 miles from the Canal, which had taken months to construct, was attacked from the air and virtually destroyed and this was followed by an assault on the oasis of Gifgafa by the Australian Light Horse after a march of 160 miles in three and a half days. The attack was completely successful and the elaborate water works which had been built up by an Austrian engineer, were demolished. These two actions so diminished the enemy's water supplies that he was compelled to draw further back. In addition a small body of British cavalry, which included squadrons from the Warwickshire and Worcestershire Yeomanry and Royal Gloucestershire Hussars, had occupied the important oasis of Katia which lies forty miles to the east of Port Said and fifty miles to the north of Gifgafa from which, however, it is separated by a range of heights, the Jebel Maghara, which were occupied by the enemy in some strength.

In the subsequent weeks there was severe fighting throughout the whole of this area, which included the Duweidar Oasis nearer to the Canal. The Turks were making constant sorties from their positions on the higher ground, and on Easter Sunday they attacked Duweidar at dawn under cover of a dense mist with a force of 2000 men. Defending the oasis was a company of Royal Scots Fusiliers who put up a stout resistance and, although sustaining heavy casualties, succeeded in holding out until they were reinforced by two more companies of the same regiment from a hill a few miles away, and eventually the Turks were routed by a bayonet charge. This action, in which both sides fought with great gallantry, was a vital one because, had Duweidar fallen, the Yeomanry also fighting against heavy odds some fifteen miles away and almost surrounded by a force of 2000 Turks and 1000 Germans and Austrians, would have been completely cut off.

There were several more encounters, which for the most part ended in favour of the British, but early in May, 1916, the Turks increased their strength in Sinai with the arrival of considerable reinforcements, probably from Gallipoli which had been evacuated by the British a few months earlier, and from a few miles away to the east of Katia were keeping a close watch on the movements of the British who were in some strength at Romani. The Turkish base was at El Arish on the coast, nearly 100 miles east of Kantara, the British base on the Canal, and by the end of June an army of about 20,000 men was concentrated there under the command of a German officer, Baron Von Kressenstein. He had by no means abandoned the idea of another direct assault on the Canal and in fact he would certainly by now have assembled a far larger striking force if it had not been for the effect produced by the Arab revolt in the Hejaz headed by Sherif Hussein of Mecca, who declared his independence of the Turks and his intention to sweep them out of Arabia.

On the 18th May, El Arish was subjected to an intense bombardment by the heavy guns of two British monitors which destroyed a fort and caused serious damage to the airfield and other installations. The camp was also set on fire in many places. The monitors were able with their shallow draught to steam very close in shore, and the Turks were so overcome by the fury of the assault that they attempted very little reply and sought shelter in the palms surrounding the camp, where they were shelled by the smaller guns of a sloop which accompanied the monitors and was able to get closer still. The attack was then taken up by several planes of the Royal Flying Corps, which dropped a number of bombs some of which exploded in the middle of a body of 1000 Turkish troops. More important still, several photographs were taken from the air which proved to be of great assistance later on. Kressenstein retaliated by bringing up to El Arish some of his anti-aircraft guns and also by making air raids during June on Kantara, Romani and other places in the vicinity of the Canal.

The assault on El Arish was followed a month later by another air raid, which was also very successful, and Kressenstein's plans were so disrupted by these attacks that he was compelled to delay his advance until late in July. In the meantime Sir Archibald Murray, who had by now succeeded Sir John Maxwell as C.-in-C., was able to complete his preparations. Permanent lines of defence were constructed from Romani to Mahemdia along the coast of the Bay of Tina, where assistance could come from the British naval forces under the command of Vice-Admiral Sir Rosslyn Wemyss.

The Turkish army, which consisted of two or three crack infantry divisions and included eight machine gun companies under German officers and partly manned by Germans, was supported by mountain artillery and batteries of four-inch and six-inch howitzers and anti-aircraft guns with Austrian gunners, and indications of the coming offensive were observed by Murray in the middle of July, with the appearance of numerous enemy aircraft over the Romani-Duweidar area. Two days later reports confirmed that the Turks were already moving westward and had reached, in considerable strength, a line stretching for some miles in a south-westerly direction from Bir-ed-Abd, about twenty miles due east of Romani, to the oasis of Magheibra.

Four companies of the Imperial Camel Corps—Nos. 6, 7, 9, and 10, which had just returned from Kharga, had now arrived in Sinai, where they were joined by two regiments of Australian Light Horse and one regiment of New Zealand Mounted Rifles to make up a formation, which was known as the Desert Mobile Column, under the overall command of Lieutenant-Colonel (later Brigadier-General) Leslie Smith, V.C. Their orders were to proceed at once to the small oasis of Bir-el-Mahadat and to establish there an advance base of operations. They did not have to wait for very long.

On the night of the 27th July, Kressenstein made an advance from Magheibra, which was temporarily checked by a New Zealand mounted regiment. In a brief skirmish the Turks lost about fifty men and it was not until the 2nd August that Kressenstein was able to make a reconnaissance in force in the direction of Katia preparatory to launching his main attack across the fifteen miles of desert which lay between his advanced troops and Romani, from where the main British defences stretched towards the coast and straddled the old caravan route, claimed to have been used by Moses in his flight from Egypt to the countries lying to the east of the Sinai Peninsula. This barren strip of desert has countless historical associations having been fought over by Egyptians, Jews, Assyrians, Babylonians, Greeks, Romans, Arabs, French and British and it was here that Napoleon's armies marched in 1799, when he advanced towards El Arish on his way to Acre.

All this time Murray was himself planning an offensive but it was not until the 3rd August that all his formations were in a position to take the field. Indeed for some hours during that day he was in doubt whether he or Kressenstein would strike first, but uncertainty came to an end when at midnight the Turks assaulted in force and drove furiously at the Romani-Mahemdia fortifications. Kressenstein's plan was to press back the British in the south, cut the railway and then attack from the rear, and for sometime it seemed as though he had succeeded. The British outposts were driven in and, when part of the line was forced, the situation began to look rather serious. About 3000 Turks made a desperate assault on two enormous sand dunes, held by the Australians and New Zealanders and, although it was repulsed, a second attack for which reinforcements had been brought up met with more success, and by the early hours of the morning both positions had fallen into enemy hands. Meanwhile the whole of the fortifications between Romani and Mahemdia had been under heavy shell fire from the howitzers and other artillery. None the less they did not make any serious impression, nor did further repeated assaults by the Turkish infantry. These attacks were made on the 52nd Division, consisting of territorials from the Lowlands of Scotland, who stood their ground and repelled the enemy at every point. Gradually the tide of battle turned and the time arrived for Murray's counter attack. Reinforcements in the shape of two mounted brigades and two brigades of the East Lancashire Territorials had now arrived on the scene and already the Turks were beginning to fall back. The two great sand dunes were recaptured with a loss of 500 men taken prisoner, a mountain battery and several machine guns, and elsewhere the Turks were beginning to sustain heavy casualties, their confusion being increased by the naval guns which caused havoc in their rear and lines of communication.

Soon they were in full retreat pursued by the cavalry and unable to make any stand until they were back again at Bir-el-Abd which they were, however, forced to evacuate three days later after being nearly surrounded. This defeat, in what came to be called the Battle of Romani, was a major disaster for the Turks, who had suffered severe losses, and it would have been worse had it not been for the intense heat and lack of water which prevented the British from pressing home their advantage, despite the many thousands of transport camels with their loads of water, food, ammunition and other supplies. Although, however, the British advance in the north was, for the time being, halted at Bir-el-Abd it was not long before the Desert Mobile Column was reformed after its exertions during the battle and was able to fulfil the principal role which had been assigned to it.

Chapter Seven

AFTER ROMANI

THE TASK of the Mobile Column was to make a detour from the south and cut into or get behind the retreating enemy and do as much damage as possible. It was rightly assumed that they could move a great deal faster than the Turks and that this would enable them not only to cut off any stragglers but also, if opportunity arose, to make attacks on the main body and at the same time have the ability to withdraw quickly into the desert should the opposition prove too strong. What actually happened was that, although the enemy lost a number of prisoners during these sorties from their flank, and were forced to abandon quantities of war material, the bulk of their forces were able to carry out a fairly orderly retreat from one prepared position to another, a series of rearguard actions being fought until they reached their strongly fortified base at El Arish.

The chief problem of the Mobile Column was, as usual in those wastes, lack of water. Wells were few and far between and most of these had been fouled or poisoned by the Turks as they retreated. In consequence the brunt of the work had to be borne by the Camel Corps, who had to make sure of the water before the cavalry could advance. Some of the wells had been filled in with sand which took several hours to clear before any water could be obtained. This would have been brackish anyway but its taste was not improved by the occasional dead camel, the pungency of the split trunks of date palms with which the wells were lined, and the chlorine which was added on the instructions of the Medical Officer! The result of all this was a highly flavoured fluid which was only fit to drink with tea. However, the Camel Corps had tremendous assets in their ability, so far as the camels were concerned, to go without water for days at a stretch, their mobility and the fact that they were able to split into self-contained units of any size as the circumstances might require. As a result the enemy were never sure of their numbers and their cavalry were afraid to pursue them in case they got cut off from their retreating main body. But whenever they had prepared positions to cover their retreat, which was naturally very slow and had to follow a fixed route from one well or waterhole to another, they made determined stands. These rearguard actions were almost continuous over a period of nearly two months and they were accompanied by three quite big engagements when the Mobile Column, which had already taken 3000 prisoners, came up with the main body. Casualties were heavy and by this time No. 10 Company alone had been reduced from a strength of five officers, 137 other ranks and 149 camels to two officers, sixty-eight other ranks and seventy-six camels.

None the less contact with the enemy had to be continually maintained and, even when it had taken several hours to dislodge them from their positions, a section or even a company of Camel Corps would be detailed for this purpose.

On one of these occasions, as a detachment of Camel Corps had been making a night march, it was discovered at dawn that one of the camels, which had been proceeding in single file, had lost its rider. There was nothing for it but to go back after him as, alone and dismounted, he would either die of thirst or be murdered by wandering Bedouin. Ashlin, who had by now assumed command of No. 10 Company, relates how he and two of his men with a spare camel went back along their tracks and, after riding for about an hour, they noticed vultures circling overhead, a sure sign that something dead or dying was near, and after a close search they discovered the missing man who was lying at the bottom of a small depression dead to the world, fast asleep. When he had fallen from his camel he must either have hit his head on a stone or been kicked by one of the other camels because he remembered nothing when he came to and was so exhausted that, regardless of his predicament, he promptly fell asleep, wisely remaining where he was. Meanwhile the vultures were all around patiently waiting for him to die. He soon recovered but he was far from popular with the two men who had accompanied Ashlin and naturally did not relish this extra ride after a long march. One of them was so disgusted, Ashlin relates, that he said to the wretched man in the broadest Yorkshire, ' We'd a' left thi to t'bloody vooltures, nobbut we s'ud a' bin sorry for t'poor bods if they'd've etten thee. Thoo'd gi'e owt t'indigestion! '

The Turks employed some of their best troops in these rearguard actions and they were helped by a number of German and Austrian officers, N.C.O.s and gunners who were attached to them. War is usually a pretty nasty affair but sometimes it brings out the best as well as the worst in those who are taking part, as the following incident will illustrate.

Major de Knoop, who was originally in command of No. 6 Company, had been put in charge of all the four Camel Corps companies at Romani and his place as O.C. No. 6 had been taken by Baron Alan de Rutzen, who was hit shortly afterwards while observing the enemy from the top of a high sand dune. He rolled down in full view of the Turks and, fully exposed as he was to intense rifle and machine gun fire, he must have been killed instantly. Attempts to reach him had to be abandoned and it was only after dark that it was possible to search for his body which, however, could not be found. The following morning a Turkish officer, waving a white flag, approached the position held by the Camel Corps, and it was assumed at first that the enemy wished to surrender, but it turned out that this was not the object of his visit. He handed over to Ashlin, who had gone out to meet him, de Rutzen's signet ring, wrist watch and some letters, which had been found in his pockets, and in excellent English said that the night before they had surprised some Bedouin stripping the dead body of a soldier which on investigation proved to be that of a British officer, and they had taken these articles from the Bedouin with the intention of handing them over to the British at the first opportunity, as they thought that the officer's family would be glad to have them. He added, as an afterthought, that they had shot the Bedouin.

Of the three engagements with the main body of the Turks two were of considerable importance and involved the whole of the Mobile Column. The first of these, which was the one in which de Rutzen lost his life, occurred on the 6th and 7th August at Hod-el-Muhamman and Hod-el-Baheir and proved to be a very sticky affair for the Camel Corps, who were ordered to occupy a position which could only be approached over a wide stretch of open ground made up of dry loose sand into which the camels sank up to their knees. In consequence the men had to dismount and lead them floundering across this open space under intense machine gun and shrapnel fire and, although they crossed in small parties, heavy casualties were sustained by men and camels alike. There were numerous acts of conspicuous gallantry. One man faced the inferno four times, in spite of being severely hit himself, and assisted in bringing in three badly wounded men and getting them under cover. Major de Knoop was hit twice, but returned each time to the firing line after having his wounds dressed, to continue directing his men. Unfortunately he did not survive the day. He was hit a third time and died before reaching the improvised first aid post.

Getting the wounded back to the Advanced Casualty Clearing Station was a serious problem for the medical staff who performed wonders. Ashlin has recalled the example set by the Senior Medical Officer, a frail, elderly man, who had been a

South of El Arish.

Bikanir Camel Corps.

Signalling by heliograph (1) on the summit of Gebel Libni.

(2) near El Arish.

Group of Bedouin in Palestine.

Turkish troops on the Jerusalem–Bethlehem Road.

German car crossing the Jordan on pontoon bridge.

No. 10 Company on the march.

(From the Theodora Duncan Collection of T. E. Lawrence.)

Part of the Hejaz Assault Column in the Wadi Rumm.
(From the Theodora Duncan Collection of T. E. Lawrence.)

The Assault Column trekking along the Hejaz railway.
(From the Theodora Duncan Collection of T. E. Lawrence.)

Turkish machine gun being used against its previous owners at Mudowra.

Pumping installation at Mudowra being destroyed.

Pumping installation at Mudowra with redoubts in background.

Typical rough country at the Wadi Ithm which had to be negotiated by
the Hejaz Assault Column.

Merlin Huth.

Captain J. J. Paterson.

Captain A. F. Newsom.
(O.C. No. 9 Company).
Killed at Amman in March 1918.

Captain C. W. Mason-MacFarlane.
(O.C. No. 8 Company).
Killed at the Baharia Oasis in September 1916.

Major F. C. Gregory, M.C. (O.C. No. 7 Company).   Killed near Jaffa in November 1917.

The Author in 1917.

Captain J. A. Lyall, M.C.
(O.C. No. 10 Company—1918).

Camels being exercised.

Lieutenant Alan F. J. Baron de Rutzen (O.C. No. 6 Company).
Killed at Romani in August 1916.

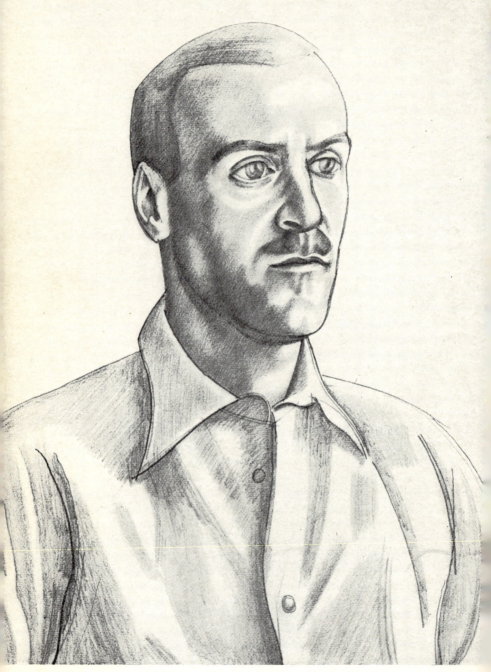

Buxton.

prominent surgeon in England, and had volunteered from one of the Yeomanry regiments with only the vaguest idea of the sort of conditions with which he would have to cope. His spirit, however, rose above physical handicaps, and those of the Camel Corps, including Ashlin himself, who passed through his hands, would always remember his great capacity for work, his gentleness, patience and unruffled calm. He was labouring under incredible difficulties as the evacuation of the wounded had to be carried out at night on camels, each animal taking two men on a kind of stretcher, called a cacolet, which was strapped on either side of the saddle.

One column of wounded sent back on the second night was put in charge of a very young and inexperienced officer who had himself been slightly wounded. By now there was such a shortage of officers that no other could be spared. Not surprisingly by morning he had completely lost his way and had it not been for a more experienced officer who, though badly hit in the chest, took charge and a severely wounded signaller who was carried to a high bit of ground and helioed for help, it is doubtful whether anybody would have survived. Fortunately the signals were picked up at Magheibra and, although subjected to several hours of blistering sun, they somehow survived the ordeal and got in safely. Meanwhile the troops in the front line were not only running very short of medical supplies but getting increasingly concerned as to the fate of the column and the message it carried. However, some twelve hours after it had been expected, a party rode in with the supplies and the welcome news of the column's safe arrival. Fortunately the fighting had practically ceased, and the Turks evacuated their positions that night. This gave a few hours of much needed rest before it was time to saddle up once more and follow the retreating enemy.

Two days later an incident occurred which was described in one of the London papers as a mounted charge by the Imperial

Camel Corps. What actually happened was this. The Camel Corps scouts suddenly came upon a small enemy ammunition and baggage column consisting of thirty pack mules, a troop of cavalry and about eighty dismounted men, who were crossing an open stretch of ground. The Camel Corps had part of two companies, approximately seventy men in all, a third of whom were ordered to dismount and give covering fire while the remainder, taking advantage of the confusion, charged in extended formation, yelling and firing their rifles from the saddle in the approved Arab style. Needless to say they did not hit anything but, although the Turks put up some slight resistance and managed to get some of their pack animals away, most of them were finally rounded up and surrendered. The result was sixty-eight prisoners taken and fourteen baggage mules. The Camel Corps casualties were two men slightly wounded and seven camels hit. Incidentally it is worth mentioning here that camels show admirable fortitude and patience, even indifference, under fire and unless badly wounded, continue as before, the slightly wounded ones showing no surprise or concern even when their nostrils are pouring blood.

The second major engagement when the Mobile Column came to grips with the Turkish main forces was at Bir-el-Bayud. Two companies of the Camel Corps, No. 9 under Lord Winterton and No. 10 under Ashlin, were operating well ahead of the Column when they ran into the southern flank-guard of the enemy. The two companies attacked at once and, after some resistance, the Turks retired on their main body, which was occupying a strong position at Bayud. There had, in fact, been some misconception on both sides. The Camel Corps were under the impression that they were up against the usual rear-guard left behind to delay their pursuers and the Turks, as it was afterwards learnt from their prisoners, thought that they were under assault from a much larger body of troops. In consequence the Turks were over-cautious and the Camel Corps over-bold. On reconnoitring they discovered their mistake and that they were confronted by a large body of troops, which outnumbered them about six to one and included several batteries of field and mountain guns.

The enemy had taken up positions on the crest of a range of fairly high sand dunes protecting a small oasis where there were some wells. The Camel Corps were well placed on a slightly higher ridge and, as it was already late in the day and the camels were tired out, and the enemy's artillery fire was doing very little harm, it was decided to remain there for the night and send back a message to Colonel Smith, who was at the advance base at Magheibra with another company of the Camel Corps. He in turn got messages through to the Australian Light Horse and the remaining Camel Corps company, instructing them to proceed at once to Bayud. Colonel Smitth arrived just after dawn with the company from Magheibra and decided to engage the enemy with the three companies on the right flank and launch the Australians, who were expected very shortly, in a determined attack from the left where there was more cover. The enemy guns were now opening up but the Camel Corps managed to occupy an advanced position, which they had been able to prepare during the night, and kept up brisk rifle and machine gun fire on the Turkish positions. Meanwhile one of the sergeants, who was a Bisley marksman, had succeeded in establishing himself, well camouflaged, on a small rise over-looking part of the Turkish line from where he did deadly execution against the enemy, killing several of them and wiping out a very troublesome machine gun nest before he was spotted and had to beat a hasty retreat. Sniping played an important part in all these operations and the snipers, who were also trained scouts, did some excellent work.

Unfortunately by noon there was still no sign of the Australians, and the Turks, who had by now got wise to the fact that they were confronted by a very small force, intensified their artillery fire and, under the cover which it provided, pushed forward two battalions with the intention of encircling the Camel Corps who were now coming under severe pressure. However, in order to complete their encircling movement, the Turks had to cross an open space where they came under heavy fire and sustained many casualties. The attack was halted but it was expected that, as soon as they had reformed, it would be resumed. Realising that the situation was becoming rather serious Colonel Smith directed one of the companies, with the spare camels, to show themselves on the summit of a hill some distance away so as to give the impression that reinforcements were approaching and, when they got down into the valley out of sight of the Turks, to double back, go round the hill, and repeat the operation several times making as much noise and raising as much dust as possible.

The ruse succeeded and it was not long before the two attacking battalions retired from such cover as they had been able to obtain and again came under heavy fire during the process. The bluff was kept up until the late afternoon when the Australians at last arrived after their forced march, but it was now too late to try and dislodge the Turks from their prepared positions, particularly as they still greatly outnumbered the combined force of Australians and Camel Corps, and the assault was postponed until the morning when further reinforcements were expected. But by then the bulk of the Turkish troops had got away with their lighter transport and all but two of their heavier guns, leaving behind their dead and a small detachment, to cover their retirement, which put up only a weak resistance and soon surrendered. The position was pretty well untenable anyway on account of the unburied corpses. In that climate the process of decomposition is very rapid. The Camel Corps had lost four officers and thirty-eight other ranks but had inflicted heavy casualties and taken 289 prisoners with a considerable quantity of equipment and the two guns.

It was during this engagement that Ashlin was wounded and

he recalls the sufferings to which the badly wounded were exposed during those grim journeys back to the Clearing Station. The distance was fifty miles and part of the travelling had to be done by day under intense heat. The flies were terrible, the water bad and insufficient and, on this occasion, the column was spotted by enemy aircraft and bombed, fortunately without doing any damage apart from adding to the general discomfort and causing further delay. The man who shared his cacolet was badly wounded and died just before the Clearing Station was reached.

It was now late September and the Camel Corps had been marching and fighting continuously for nearly two months. The Turks were in full retreat towards their base at El Arish but it was not until the 21st December that this was at last occupied by the advancing British forces. During these operations, and the fierce engagements which followed at Maghdaba on the 23rd December and Rafa on the 9th January, units of the Camel Corps, which included, in addition to the Australians and New Zealanders, Nos. 6, 7, and 9 Companies of the 2nd Battalion, played an outstanding part.

Maghdaba lies about twenty-five miles to the south of El Arish and its capture was described in a dispatch from Mr W. T. Massey, one of the British war correspondents, as a brilliant stroke, made under extraordinarily arduous conditions, which resulted in an overwhelming defeat of the Turkish garrison by the mounted troops of the desert column, under the command of Lieutenant-General Sir H. Chauvel, and a victory much more far-reaching than the capture of 1300 prisoners would indicate. ' This swift fierce and irresistible attack,' said Mr Massey, ' has produced one of the most important effects of the campaign in Egypt. The sudden rush of mounted troops, twenty-five miles from El Arish, a distance which by all previous experience of desert warfare was considered impossible in a single night, has had an immense moral influence on the Turks whose calculations

in Northern Sinai were completely upset—thus the victory at
Maghdaba, which added fame to the Anzac Mounted Division
and proved the sterling value of the Imperial Camel Corps
drawn from British yeomanry and colonial regiments, may be
regarded as one of the most important battles of the campaign
in Eastern Egypt.'

The Turks were well entrenched in the form of a rough
circle 3500 yards in diameter with five large closed works or
redoubts. The attack was launched at 8 a.m. The Camel Corps,
supported by its own mountain battery and the guns of the
Territorial Horse Artillery, began the frontal assault while the
Anzac Mounted Division, under the command of Brigadier-
General E. W. C. Chaytor, moved north of the Turkish positions,
under cover of the sand dunes to the east and south east of
Maghdaba, to cut off the retreat of the enemy. The battle
lasted for eight hours and has been described as being of a
desperate character with the Turks offering the most strenuous
resistance from the protection of their redoubts.

Shortly after the troops moved off aeroplane messages indicated that some of the enemy were retiring, and the mounted
brigades on the east of Maghdaba pushed on quickly so as to
complete the envelopment while a reserve brigade was sent
forward to assist in the movement. It was soon discovered,
however, that only small bodies of the enemy were withdrawing
towards their main positions, which were still held in considerable strength. The reserve brigade came under heavy machine
gun fire and the other brigades were systematically shelled by
the enemy's Krupp mountain guns.

Meanwhile the Camel Corps were also receiving attention
from the enemy's guns as they moved across the open plain
towards the redoubts, without their line of approach affording
the slightest vestige of cover. However, to quote Mr Massey
again they continued to advance ' with magnificent steadiness '.

The reserve brigade, unable to go forward without further

serious losses among its horses, swung to its flank to assist in the
frontal assault which was beginning to slow down in places.
One of the redoubts was blown to pieces but the others succeeded
in maintaining their fire, the British gunners being hampered
by mirage and the flat nature of the ground which prevented
the establishment of forward observation posts. However, in
the early afternoon the advance was resumed all along the line,
and during the next two hours the fighting reached its greatest
intensity. Aircraft attacked the redoubts, the guns increased
their fire and the troopers, dismounting, joined with the Camel
Corps in making repeated assaults.

A further danger appeared when it was reported that no water
could be found so that, unless the position could be taken before
the end of the day, the thirsty troops and their thirstier mounts
would be forced to withdraw to El Arish. So the order was
given to push the attack with all possible speed and from then
onward the pressure was increased at all points. A detachment
of Australian Light Horse on the enemy's left captured a small
redoubt to the west of the enemy's position taking 100 prisoners.
A little later two regiments of Light Horse were within 200
yards on the north east and in touch with the Camel Corps
coming in from the north west. The New Zealand Mounted
Rifles were also within reach of their objective. Half an hour
later the second line of defence had come under attack from the
combined forces and one of the main redoubts was carried after
a dashing charge, all its occupants including the Turkish commandant being taken prisoner. Immediately afterwards another
detachment of Light Horse charged, mounted, with the bayonet
and soon after 4 p.m. what were left of the gallant Turkish
defenders had surrendered.

But it was not long before the desert column was to be called
on for further exertions. On the 27th December reports were
received from the air reconnaissance that the Turks were pre-
paring a strongly entrenched position at Magruntein covering

the little town of Rafa, thirty miles east of El Arish and on the Sinai and Palestine border. Although the position was of no particular strategic value it was felt that it would be bad policy to allow its fortification to be completed, and on the night of the 8th January Lieutenant-General Sir Philip Chetwode commanding the desert column, which again consisted of a mounted division of Australians and New Zealanders, the Imperial Camel Corps, the Territorial Horse Artillery and some British Yeomanry set out from El Arish and, covering the distance in only twelve hours, launched the attack at dawn on the 9th January, the Turks being once more completely taken by surprise by the swiftness of the British advance coming so soon after the capture of Maghdaba.

For its size the Turkish position was formidable. Three series of works, facing south-east, south-west and west, were connected by trenches dominated by a redoubt 2000 yards west of Rafa. In addition on all sides the ground was so level as almost to constitute a *glacis* and without cover of any kind for the advancing troops. However, the guns soon began to register hits and, after a heavy bombardment, the New Zealand Rifles attacked the eastern defences, with the Australian Light Horse on their left and the Camel Corps coming in from the south. By 11 a.m. these defences had been taken with a loss to the enemy of 160 prisoners in addition to killed and wounded, and Rafa itself was in British occupation.

But there still remained the strong south-western and western defences and the main redoubt itself. Soon after mid-day the attacking troops had been redeployed and while the New Zealanders and Australians mounted a fresh assault from the south-west the Camel Corps and Yeomanry attacked from the west. Very soon the entire position was encircled apart from a small gap to the north-west but the Horse Artillery dashed forward to support the attack at close quarters and by 2 p.m. the gap had been closed.

At 3.30 p.m. a message was received from the air force that a
large column of relieving Turkish troops was approaching from
the east and General Chetwode ordered a general attack to be
made on the redoubt by all the available forces and pressed
home to the utmost, leaving the relief column to the attentions
of the aircraft. Spurred on by the need for speed the storming
parties, splendidly supported by the gunners, burst into the
redoubt and by 5.30 p.m., just ten hours after the action had
started, the Turks at last conceded defeat and surrendered. A
small force was detailed to assist the aircraft in dealing with the
relief column which was soon dispersed.

In the whole of this operation the British had sustained 487
casualties of which seventy-one were killed while the Turks,
in addition to about 600 killed and wounded, had lost thirty-five
officers and 1600 men taken prisoner. They had also lost several
guns and a quantity of other equipment.

The engagements at Maghdaba and Rafa were followed in
March and April by two attempts to assault and capture the town
of Gaza, but the Turks, who occupied strongly fortified positions,
put up a very stout resistance, and on both occasions the British
forces, which included the 52nd, 53rd and 54th infantry divisions
in addition to the desert column, were beaten back and, after
sustaining heavy casualties, compelled to withdraw from the
ground they had gained during the early stages of the fighting.

Chapter Eight

SOLLUM

It is now time to return to No. 8 Company which at the end of January, 1917, was on its way back to Abbassia after the completion of the Baharia operations.

The few weeks we spent at Abbassia were relatively uneventful. We had hoped that at the end of this period of refitting and retraining we would be sent to the Palestine front but as it turned out we had not yet finished with the Western Desert, where the Senussi war was now in its closing stages. Our destination this time was Sollum to which we proceeded by way of Alexandria, Alamein, Daba, Mersa Matruh, Sidi Barrani and other places which were to become famous in another war. It was a season of sudden sandstorms and alternations of heat and cold which at times became almost intolerable. At Mersa Matruh where we stayed for several days I had the misfortune to be thrown by one of my camels and, although not seriously injured, I hurt my back rather badly. The camel was a lively creature at the best of times, but on this occasion I found him quite uncontrollable. The camel lines were located just outside the barbed-wire perimeter and the camel had been brought in through the gate to the officers' quarters which were just inside. The moment I mounted and made for the gate the camel took charge and galloped straight at the barbed wire which was about fifteen feet wide. I suppose I loosened my grip with the intention of dismounting if I got the chance but, whatever the reason, I was flung in the air and landed flat on my back. I can just remember the animal floundering about in the middle of the wire before I more or less lost consciousness and was removed on a stretcher. It was a pretty nasty fall from which I did not fully recover for some weeks.

On our arrival at Sollum we found that patrolling was still going on, and the last in which I took part turned out to be quite an exciting one. I only had five or six men with me and my orders were to make a five-day reconnaissance, first of all due west to the Libyan frontier, then south as far as we could go in the time, then east and north so as to reach the sea on the evening of the fourth day and then back to Sollum along the coast. The coastal district is bounded by an escarpment several hundred feet high which converges on the sea as you travel west, and Sollum lies at the point where it reaches the sea.

First of all, therefore, we had to climb the escarpment by a rough track which led up from the camp, and after that we would be remaining on the high ground until we hit the escarpment again several miles to the east and a couple of miles or so from the sea. Unfortunately during the whole of the time the sky was covered by heavy cloud, and it was impossible to take any bearings from the sun or the stars. I, therefore, had to rely on my compass, which I distrusted anyway because it always seemed to differ from my own ideas! In fact when the time came to make our first change of direction to the south I was almost convinced that the compass was wrong, and for the remainder of the patrol I was in a state of considerable anxiety that we might be heading in the wrong direction, with what could only be a disastrous result. Whether it was due to the humidity in the atmosphere or to some other reason there was a constant succession of mirages which made everything seem very unreal. Once or twice we came across a solitary Arab who passed us without a word and with hardly a glance. Otherwise the desert was or seemed to be nothing but an empty wilderness of rock and sand. Sometime during the third day, however,

when we must have been at our farthest point, we rounded a
range of hillocks which had for some time obscured our view on
that side and saw to our consternation a large Bedouin encampment about a quarter of a mile away. There was no chance of
taking cover as they had already seen us and we could see and
hear a lot of rushing about, with dogs barking and men shouting
and, what was more alarming, running for their camels. Equally
disconcerting was the realisation that the encampment was
exactly in the direction in which we were heading. This was
obviously an occasion for discretion rather than valour, and for
testing the speed of our camels. They responded nobly, probably
because they were almost as scared as we were by all the sudden
commotion, and we soon began to draw away from our pursuers, who eventually dropped out of sight. By then we were
badly off our course in addition to which we were continually
changing direction in case the Bedouin had not given up the
chase, and by the time we camped for the night, about twenty
miles farther on, I for one had not the remotest idea where we
were. However, the immediate objective was not to get caught
and, although I do not know whether the Bedouin were Senussi
or their friends, all the Arabs in that region were hostile and none
of us cared very much for the idea of falling into their hands.

There was no incident during the night and the following
morning I decided that, wherever we were, the time had come
to turn north in the general direction of the Mediterranean.
We started early and kept going all day. By mid-day we were
all, including the camels, pretty tired and thirsty and there was
still no sign of a break. But in the late afternoon for no apparent
reason the camels suddenly started to perk up a bit and lengthen
their stride, although it was not until some time later that we were
able to detect a freshness in the air which could only mean the sea.

This was a great relief in more ways than one, especially to
myself. I could only hope that I had succeeded in disguising
from my companions the fact that I really had not had a clue

as to our position for at any rate the last two days. Eventually
we reached the edge of the escarpment and looked down on the
sea a few miles away. We could see no way down and I decided
to camp for the night. The camels were unloaded and unsaddled,
the blankets were spread, our cook began to prepare a meal and
we all prepared to settle down for a good night's rest when
suddenly we were attacked not by Arabs but by ticks!

There were thousands of them coming at us from all directions.
In a moment they were climbing up our legs on to our bare
knees and then up the length of our bodies. We were all yelling
and swearing, the camels were bellowing, and if there was an
Arab within ten miles he must have heard us. We seemed to be
at the hub of a wheel of which the spokes were long black lines
of these revolting little crablike creatures, much bigger than an
ordinary sheep tick. I had often heard of what an army of ants
can do in some parts of the world, but an invasion of ticks was
something quite new. Our bodies were crawling with them
and within minutes they had even reached our necks and hair.
During our training we used to have exercises in loading up and
making a quick getaway from, so to speak, a standing start, but
I am willing to bet that on this occasion all records were com-
fortably beaten when we cleared out of that horrible place. I
have earlier described how after a meal of blood the ticks used
to hang from the camels like obscene bunches of grapes, and we
were in no mood to test what would be the effect on the human
body. So we carried on along the escarpment for another
mile or two and were fortunate enough to find a gap which was
not too steep for us to take the camels down to sea-level, where
we thankfully set up our camp once more without a tick in sight.
The next day we proceeded by easy stages along the few miles
back to Sollum, where we were thankful to have our first wash,
shave and change of clothes for five days.

The track up the escarpment at Sollum was a pretty rough
sort of affair and we had to take out working parties to try and

improve it. I have often wondered whether this was the site of Halfaia Pass which became so well known to the Eighth Army during the Second War. Probably not, but in those days it was the only track which existed.

We had a rather humorous incident at Sollum. An Italian cruiser had anchored in the bay (the Italians were, of course, our allies in the First War) and they sent out two boats with an enormous net like a seine to see whether they could get any fish. When the boats landed and they started to pull in the net it was soon apparent that their efforts were going to be successful. The sea was literally boiling with fish which turned out to be a shoal of barracuda, and as they were brought nearer to land the Italian sailors became so excited that they seemed to have some difficulty in collecting the catch. In this, however, they were helped by the British and from every unit in the camp there could be observed a mess corporal sauntering towards the beach with a large sack over his shoulder. Undaunted by screams of rage and shaking of fists by the Italians the corporals walked into the seething mass of fish and filled up their sacks, and then calmly retraced their steps to their respective kitchens. There was really no reason why our allies should have been so angry, because their boats were already so full of fish that they nearly sank on their way back to the cruiser, but angry they certainly were and their gestures were quite unmistakable. And in any case the corporals were only putting into practice one of the basic precepts of their training, namely to show initiative and enterprise on every possible occasion, and I doubt very much whether they regarded the possibility of their actions leading to an international incident as being in any way their concern.

That is the last thing I can remember of Sollum because a week or two later the news for which we had been waiting and hoping for so long came at last. We were to leave the Western Desert and join the army which was facing the Turks in Palestine.

Before leaving the Senussi campaign, however, there is one

more story I should like to relate in a rather lighter vein, for which I am indebted to certain characters in No. 10 Company, which had come up from the Kharga and Dahkla oases to relieve us at Sollum.

On the eatern tip of the Gulf of Sollum there is a place called Bag-Bag. It is, or was, almost nothing at all, a pile of glaring white sand-dunes with a very brackish well. A mile away there was a Bedouin encampment whose Sheikh, a one-eyed old gentleman, about eighty years of age, was known as Sidi Barrani and who was paid a retainer in return for tipping off the British whenever a supply column was attempting to get through to the Senussi in Cyrenaica. The Bedouin were particularly attracted to the Medical Service and Sidi Barrani asked for something to relieve the constipation from which he habitually suffered. He was given a handful of ' Number Nines ', well known to every British soldier in the First War, and he subsequently reported that they were indeed ' most powerful medicine ' !

Whether or not it was in gratitude for this deliverance he afterwards, as a great honour, invited some of the cameliers to witness the circumcision of his son, aged six. (If he was indeed eighty years old he must have been a remarkable old man!) There was a great feast and the members of the tribe, including both sexes and all ages, danced round the fires singing and shouting and banging gongs. Suddenly ' before our very eyes ' the Sheikh ed Din (or the Ulema) performed the operation ' neat ' with a well whetted old French table knife! The cameliers were asked to testify that those outside the tent heard no cry from the very brave boy, which they were able to do quite truthfully because the din drowned his screams! Then the Ulema took some darkish powder from a bag and flung it over the wound. Later that night the mother of the boy sent over and asked for the ' Doctor ' and some of the men went over with the R.A.M.C. corporal, who had provided the old man with his ' most powerful medicine ' and he cleaned and dressed the poor little chap properly. It transpired that the darkish powder, which had been hoped would congeal the blood, was finely ground coffee!

Sidi Barrani once related that, during the Senussi occupation, a German officer in gorgeous white uniform and a ' gold ' helmet visited him and prayed with the Faithful. He understood that the Germans were an Islamic nation and that they were being called upon to respond to a Jehad (Holy War). It was explained to him that in fact the Reformed Christian religion had begun in Germany where there were no Moslems. In the British Empire, on the other hand, there were millions of good Moslems and many of them were fighting the Turks side by side with the Christians. Let us hope that Sidi Barrani was duly impressed!

Chapter Nine

EL ARISH

OUR IMMEDIATE destination was El Arish and this involved a pretty long journey. First of all we had to trek all the way back to Alexandria which took several days, then we had to proceed by rail to Kantara, which was the principal base on the Suez Canal for the military operations in Palestine, and finally, also by rail, to El Arish There were three lines of communication through Sinai from Kantara to the front, consisting of the railway, a meshed wire track to facilitate marching over the sand and, last but not least, the water pipeline on which the army's existence virtually depended, and which was continually subject to raids by Turkish cavalry patrols for the purpose of cutting out sections of the line.

We reached El Arish in mid-June, 1917, just before the arrival in Egypt of General Sir Edmund Allenby, who had been sent out to take over the command of the army from Sir Archibald Murray. It was a rather critical time because, after the two attempts to capture Gaza had failed, the morale of the army was at a rather low ebb and there was a general feeling of listlessness and depression.

Allenby's arrival was like a breath of fresh air, which was soon to take on the dimensions of a gale, and Mr Brian Gardner has recorded in his book *Allenby*, published by Cassell in 1965, how the first section of the army to feel the draught was G.H.Q. itself and that a number of staff officers who had been spending much time propping up the bar at Shepheard's Hotel soon found themselves on a boat home, as did a few elderly regimental colonels and one divisional commander.

Except for the divisional commander I can confirm this from my own personal experience because, as it happens, I paid a visit to Shepheard's a few months before Allenby's arrival and again a short time afterwards, and the difference was truly amazing. I have never seen such an array of brass gathered together as I found in the bars and dining-rooms on the first occasion, nor so few as on my second visit. The removal of all this dead wood made a tremendous impression on the army's morale and incidentally it was the first time I ever heard the expression ' being given the order of the bowler hat '.

One of the first things that Allenby did was to carry out his expressed intention of visiting as many of the forward troops as it was humanly possible to do, and the day came when, although we were still in reserve, it was announced that he was going to inspect us. This turned out to be quite a memorable encounter. We were drawn up in line mounted on our camels when we saw a cloud of dust which heralded the approach of half a dozen horsemen proceeding at full gallop towards a point about a quarter of a mile to our front. Leading the posse was a gigantic man mounted on a gigantic horse, who could not possibly have been mistaken for anybody but our new commander-in-chief. On arrival at the point he swung round his horse and galloped straight at the centre of our line and did not pull up until he was about fifty yards away. And there he sat and we looked at each other What he thought of us I cannot say but certainly we had none of us ever seen anybody or anything quite so impressive. Camels and horses have a natural antipathy and they are always very uneasy in each other's company. Certainly our camels had shown unmistakable signs of their nervousness and distrust at the approach of this giant equestrian figure out of the blue and the noise of their complaining filled the air. Fortunately, however, they were all equally affected so that although they backed several yards they maintained a straight line. After the inspection Allenby insisted on speaking personally to each of the officers and we all dismounted and went up to him in turn. He leant down, shook us by the hand, said a few words of encouragement and departed, as he had come, in a cloud of dust followed by his staff. The next time I saw him was a year later when I was in hospital in Alexandria.

Our life in El Arish was rather pleasant. There was a lot of refitting and re-equipping to be done before we could be ready to take part in the campaign which Allenby was planning for the autumn, and our duties were confined to patrolling the surrounding areas. Some of these were carried out at company strength and lasted for several days, but the one which I recollect most clearly was quite a small patrol, which I had to take out to a place called Gebel Libni in the Sinai Desert in order to determine whether this would be a suitable location for the establishment of a heliograph station.

Gebel Libni was about two days' march away. It was a curious and vaguely sinister rock formation more than 1000 feet high. It had no particular peak but there were dozens of pinnacles pointing like fingers to the sky and there were several caves and crevices leading right into the centre of the formation, which stood out against the flatness of the surrounding desert like a black and monstrous growth. There seemed to be something evil about the place which was in no way decreased by the fact that it was the home of hordes of vultures. As we approached it in the late evening we disturbed a desert hare which jumped out of a bush of some kind, probably camel thorn, and ran off into the desert. Immediately a vulture detached itself from one of the pinnacles and a few moments later it swooped down on the running hare and started to climb again very slowly with the wretched animal in its talons. Somebody fire a rifle at it and it dropped the hare and flew back to its pinnacle squawking with rage. When we picked it up the hare was quite dead, not only from the fall, but the fearful wounds inflicted by the talons. We had it for dinner and it was delicious. The whole time it was being skinned, cleaned, cooked and eaten we were watched by the vulture and his friends who occupied every point of vantage on the rocks. After dinner I thought I would try and shoot one with a rifle. It was a long shot, about 200 yards, and when I saw a puff of feathers and dust where the bullet struck the rock just behind it I thought I had succeeded. However, it flew away apparently unharmed. Later on I walked up to the rocks and into one of the crevices, but it was a horrible place and I was glad to get back to my companions.

Next day we climbed up to a sort of plateau quite near the top which seemed to be about the only place where we could set up the heliograph apparatus. To one side of this there was a vulture's eyrie, which was very little more than a circular depression about eight feet in diameter. It was covered with droppings, blood and bits of skin and bones, the relics no doubt of many a delightful meal, and it stank to high heaven. We did not want to stay there longer than we had to, especially with all those horrible birds watching us from the surrounding rocks, and I for one was very relieved when our signallers succeeded in establishing helio contact with the next observation post, which I estimated to be at least thirty miles away. I was afterwards told that it was nearer sixty. I took a photograph of the place which I still have and whether through some fault in the film or the exposure, or for some other reason, it seems to be overshadowed by a vast and brooding figure. Perhaps it was there all the time. I can well believe it!

Our recreations at El Arish included bathing and cricket. In June the water is beginning to get very warm and, in fact, we found it almost too warm and in consequence rather enervating. However, it was pleasant and we usually took the camels into the sea with us and gave them a good scrubbing, the last they were to have for many a long day. Cricket in the cool of the evening, played on a coconut matting pitch, was delightful and we had several matches against a British West Indian regiment, which happened to be camped near by.

El Arish had a large population of chameleons and we had several of these fascinating little creatures for pets. They certainly lived up to their reputation for changing colour and merging into the background. They also helped enormously to keep down the flies, which they collected at the end of their darting tongues in vast quantities. Tortoises too were always wandering about the camp, and I was woken one morning by a little jerboa sitting on my chest and gazing at me intently with its saucer-like eyes. Very foolishly I put out my hand to touch it and it promptly bit one of my fingers to the bone.

One other thing which I remember at this time was that the name of Lawrence was coming into prominence, and we were officially warned against shooting at any strangers without making due enquiry first, as it was believed that he was somewhere in the vicinity on one of his mysterious missions and, as was his invariable custom, dressed as an Arab.

Whether this report was true I cannot say but I certainly never met up with him myself. In fact, so far as I am aware, the first member of the Camel Corps to encounter Lawrence was Laurence Moore, whose No. 10 Company returned in August from Sollum, where it had been relieved by No. 6 Company, and rejoined the Imperial Camel Brigade.

At some time during the operations which are described in the next chapter two of the New Zealand companies were sent on a reconnaissance mission into the Negev, the desert area running from Beersheba down to the Gulf of Akaba, and Moore had orders to fix up a line of heliograph stations to cover them.

This is his account of what happened.

I was visiting one of these stations one day when the look-out reported a group of about half a dozen Arabs approaching from the south east, the approximate direction of Akaba. We signalled

them to come in and I was sent forward, as interpreter, to inter-
rogate them. I called out in my very sketchy Arabic ' Who are
you—where are you from—where are you going?' but realised
that this was unnecessary when I saw that their leader was obviously
a European, who had made no attempt at disguise beyond the fact
that he wore Arab clothing. A fair smallish built man with rather
a large head, clothed in a brown Arab *aba* covering an immaculately
white undergarment: on his head he wore a cream coloured
kuffieyeh, the usual Arab headcloth held down by a double twisted
agal or headrope (which the Arab takes off at night and uses to
hobble his camel's legs, whereas each of our camels carried a rope
round his neck which we used for the same purpose). The *agal*
of this obvious European was made of black wool and the stiffening
pieces were bound in gold wire. We had vaguely heard of a
British officer doing marvellous things with a force of Arab guer-
rillas somewhere away to our right and we had been warned of the
possibility of his appearance in our vicinity, and sure enough this
was the man. He introduced himself as (I think) Captain Lawrence
and asked to be taken to Descorps, the H.Q. of Desert Mounted
Corps. I could not go all the way back with him but I did ride
with him the greater part of the day as far as the H.Q. of the Imperial
Camel Brigade, commanded by Brigadier-General Leslie Smith, V.C.

During the course of the march I listened in very intently and
was able to follow most of the conversation. Lawrence was
obviously treating most of his companions as equals and I discovered later that they were minor sherifs, representing the King
of the Hejaz, and on their way to be presented to G.H.Q. They
had one or two servants with them and I chatted with them quite
freely, mostly about the problems of the immediate march, and
all the time I was most anxious to ask Lawrence how one could get
into his outfit. I did not realise it at the time but in point of fact
we *were* in his outfit from that day on. He had come across to see
Allenby about the possibility of a link between the British right
and the Arab army away to the east. As things turned out later on
it was we, the Camel Corps, who were to help provide the link.

Chapter Ten

PALESTINE—ADVANCE ON JERUSALEM

WE STAYED at El Arish until the end of September when we began moving forward to take up our positions for the attack on the Gaza Beersheba line which was planned for the end of October and in which virtually the whole of the Camel Brigade was to become involved as part of the newly formed Desert Mounted Corps, which also included four cavalry divisions, under the command of an Australian, Lieutenant-General Sir H. Chauvel.

The remainder of the army had also been reorganised, since the arrival from England of subtsantial reinforcements, into 20th Corps, consisting of four infantry divisions and four brigades of heavy artillery, under the command of Lieutenant-General Sir P. W. Chetwode, and 21st Corps, consisting of three infantry divisions and three brigades of heavy artillery, under the command of Lieutenant-General E. S. Bulfin. For the forthcoming operations, therefore General Allenby had at his disposal a force of nearly 100,000 men with an effective fighting strength of about 75,000. Against this the Turks had only 35,000 men in the line but the enormous superiority of the British was largely counter-balanced by the strength of the Turkish positions and the general nature of the country which lent itself easily to defence.

On the 15th October I celebrated my twenty-first birthday

but I cannot remember exactly where we were. My fellow officers, including those from No. 7 Company commanded by Major Gregory, did their best for me and somebody had managed to arrange for a case of beer to be sent up from somewhere in the rear. We sat down to a splendid repast and the first bottle was opened. Directly the stopper was removed there was a minor explosion and a stream of foam shot up to the top of the tent, and ran down the sides. Nor did it stop until the bottle was empty. Without a word being spoken each of the remaining bottles was opened in turn and behaved in exactly the same way, not one of them yielding a single drop to drink.

Gregory was a splendid man. Although I think he was British by birth he had spent most of his life abroad in search of adventure and when war broke out he was pearl fishing somewhere near the Great Barrier Reef off the coast of Queensland. I had first met him when I was on a course in England and we were billeted together in the same house. I had formed a great admiration for him and he had already made his mark as a soldier and natural leader with a tremendous driving force. It was a great loss to the Camel Corps when he was killed a few weeks later.

Very soon after my birthday we moved up to a place called Khalasa, which was about fifteen miles south of Beersheba and on the extreme right flank of the line. Moore has made the point that the reason why the Camel Corps was deployed on the right—as had also been the case at Romani—was apparently due to the simple but erroneous belief on the part of G.H.Q. that, because the camels could go for several days without water, their riders could do the same! In consequence of this delusion they suffered badly from thirst in comparison with the infantry, who as a general rule occupied the coastal regions where water, though brackish, was plentiful, and the cavalry in the central section where there were also a few wells, the Camel Corps being left to enjoy the amenities of a burning desert where there were hardly any wells at all. However, it must be admitted that this was precisely the sort of country for which it had been trained.

Despite the lateness of the year there was a heat wave which lasted several days with temperatures of up to 110°. This was nearly my undoing. I had been on outpost duty since dawn under a pitiless sun and spent most of the day staring through binoculars in the general direction of the enemy lines, and catching an occasional glimpse of a Turkish cavalry patrol. I can only describe the desert on that occasion as a shimmering white-hot furnace and, as the day wore on, I began to feel pretty awful, with a blinding headache which got worse and worse until it was time to withdraw and report back to Battalion H.Q. I used to suffer badly from migraine, and this sort of thing had happened to me once or twice before, but never so severely as this. For some reason I was temporarily in command of the company and I remember Lord Winterton coming out of his tent to instruct me on the dispositions we were to make for the night. I was feeling so ill by then that I did not hear, or at any rate, take in a word he said and it was fortunate that I had my C.S.M., Sergeant-Major Guppy, with me at the time. A few moments after Lord Winterton walked away I collapsed and spent the next quarter of an hour lying on the ground and being violently sick. They got me away eventually and for the next three days I lay under a ground sheet with a sharp attack of sunstroke, and with the knowledge imparted to me by the M.O. that, unless I recovered by the time we were to move forward, I would have to be evacuated to hospital. Fortunately I made it. Our orders came through on the third evening, and although I was still pretty shaky I was allowed to rejoin the company in time for its departure on the following morning.

A day or two later we took up our final position to the west of Beersheba, and at the end of October the attack which was to result a few weeks later in the capture of Jerusalem was launched on the Turkish positions. It seems that the Turkish, or rather German High Command, under General von Falkenhayn, was in two minds as to whether the main attack would be delivered at Gaza or Beersheba. Gaza seemed to be the more likely, and it had already been subjected to an intense artillery bombardment, supported by guns from Allied warships. But in fact Allenby had decided that the main, or at any rate, the initial offensive should be directed at Beersheba. If successful this would mean that the whole of the Turkish line could be turned from its eastern and unprotected flank and Gaza itself would become virtually untenable. This is precisely what happened. The attack on Beersheba was made by 20th Corps and Desert Mounted Corps, and one of its main features was the charge of a brigade of Australian Light Horse, which overran the Turkish defences and ended in the capture of the vitally important wells before they could be demolished. Prior to this the town had been subjected to a heavy bombardment by our guns which preceded an attack by the infantry from the west and south. My company was in reserve at this stage and we were interested observers of the bombardment as the guns were stretched out on either side of us, and we could see the Turkish positions a mile or so away erupting in a solid mass of exploding shells. For some reason which I cannot explain, but probably with the idea of calming our excitement over our first contact with real war, Lord Winterton took the opportunity during a brief pause to deliver a lecture to some of the junior officers, including myself, on the subject of parliamentary procedure!

Later that day we entered Beersheba and reached the railway station which was apparently deserted. There were a number of railway wagons in a siding and several of the men rushed forward to see what they could find. Fortunately we stopped them just in time. The wagons turned out to be a vast booby trap. They were packed with explosives which were wired to the doors. Had any of these been opened the whole contraption would have gone up in an explosion which would not only have destroyed us all, but most of what was left of Beersheba as well. This was an extremely lucky escape as I do not think that we would have thought of booby traps at all if it had not been for an incident which occurred a few minutes earlier when one of the men picked up a bottle of beer, which was lying a few yards away, with fatal results to himself. It turned out afterwards that practically every object of interest in that particular area was a trap. Somebody had certainly been busy.

It would be convenient at this point to mention that on the 30th October, the day before the attack on Beersheba, Colonel S. F. Newcombe's party which consisted of seventy men from No. 5 Company Imperial Camel Corps, a detachment of sixteen men from the 21st London Regiment of the 60th Division and some Arab scouts, moved into the desert east of the town with the object of raising the local Bedouin in revolt against the Turks at the moment of Allenby's offensive, and blocking the road north to Hebron and Jerusalem after Beersheba had fallen. The party was exceptionally strong in fire power for its size, being armed with ten heavy machine guns in addition to a number of Lewis guns and explosives.

In his book 'T. E. Lawrence'—In Arabia and After, which was first published by Jonathan Cape in 1934, the late Sir Basil Liddell Hart described the effect on the Turkish High Command when, on the evening of the 31st October, Newcombe and his men moved down to the Beersheba-Hebron road and cut the telegraph line to Jerusalem. In fact it spread such alarm behind the Turkish lines that, in the enemy's imagination, the bulk of the British Army could only be advancing north of the Hebron road and straight for Jerusalem. In consequence they not only dispatched their one division in general reserve towards Hebron but also drew off reserves from the Sheria sector to meet the supposed threat to their left flank.

Newcombe's hopes of a rising by the Bedouin were, however, disappointed as they preferred to wait on events before committing themselves. Furthermore there was no sign of the hoped for advance by British cavalry to his relief and, as the hours slipped away, his chances of extricating his little party were becoming more and more remote.

On the 1st November an attack by about 100 Turks was repulsed with loss but Liddell Hart describes how, on the next morning, converging forces of the enemy from Hebron and Dhariyeh succeeded in clearing away the obstructions, which for forty hours had disrupted all communications with Jerusalem, and, after twenty of his men had been killed, many others wounded and most of his machine guns disabled during the ensuing battle, Newcombe was forced to surrender when the Turks, who were under German command, had reached positions from which they would have been able to shoot down all the survivors. It could be argued that he had been unwise not to withdraw a few hours earlier while the way was still open. Be that as it may, however, the entire operation had shown a magnificent example of initiative, courage and determination and perhaps it would be true to say that even the loss of those brave men was outweighed by the almost panic effect on the morale of the Turks and the consequent interference with the dispositions they had made in the face of Allenby's general offensive following the capture of Beersheba. This is shown by the fact that, on the evening of Newcombe's surrender, no less than two Turkish divisions and two cavalry regiments were deployed in the hills near the Hebron road with a third division on the way. And there they remained to take part in a series of ineffective actions on the British Army's flank until on the 6th November Chetwode's divisions crashed into and through the Sheria defences where only two Turkish regiments had been left to hold six miles of front.

I cannot help feeling that in the story of the Imperial Camel

Corps this episode must surely rank as one of its finer achievements.

I must now pick up the threads of my main narrative. After the fall of Beersheba the Turks had to some extent reorganised and begun to take up positions to the north and north-west, and a day or two later the 53rd Division and part of Desert Mounted Corps including ourselves, were faced with the Turkish 19th Division at a place called Tel Khuweilfe. Although it was now November the heat was unbearable with the temperature officially 107° in the shade, but there was no shade. The day before Khuweilfe was taken my company lay out under the blazing sun from early morning to dusk without any water at all. There was virtually no cover and the slightest movement attracted the attention of a Turkish battery posted on higher ground. As the day wore on things began to look rather serious. Our throats and lips were parched and our tongues became swollen and blackened, and some of the men were in really bad shape. We opened tins of peas and marmalade and drank, if you can call it drinking, the hot grease and vegetable matter, which did not really help very much. I had a flask of brandy with me and although it would, of course, have been fatal to drink any I found some relief from moistening my lips and then sucking them. A rumour had gone round that the wells at Beersheba had not been captured intact after all and that in any case the water had been poisoned. I do not think that there was any truth in this, but certainly the delay in bringing up a supply of water did nothing to discourage it. However, that evening, a convoy of camel transport with water tanks did succeed in making its way to the front-line area, but it was only just in time. Had it arrived a few hours later there could have been a real disaster and, as it was, the convoy was rushed by members of an infantry unit who had been without water for the best part of two days, and were driven almost mad with thirst. This only resulted in a lot of the precious liquid being wasted, but eventually the water reached its various destinations and the situation was restored. But if there had been further delay, or had the Turks been able to counter-attack and destroy the convoy, something like two and perhaps three divisions would have been put out of action. This was a truly horrible day.

The next day we passed through Khuweilfe which was littered with Turkish corpses already in an advanced state of decomposition. By this time Gaza itself had been captured and the whole of the Turkish forces were in retreat, although far from being demoralised. In fact, considering what they had been called upon to endure (the bombardment of Gaza alone from land and sea had lasted for four days) they were still fighting with tremendous courage and tenacity and there was no semblance of a rout. In defence the Turks are as good fighters as any in the world (as they showed in the Korean War) and I think that everyone was full of admiration for the stubbornness with which they conducted their retreat, although exposed to a series of dazzling cavalry charges by the Yeomanry and Australian Light Horse. After Khuweilfe, Desert Mounted Corps and the 60th Division executed a turning movement to the north-west in the general direction of Huj and Askalon, which is on the sea. The days seemed to pass very rapidly and after all this time my recollections are somewhat blurred, but I can vividly remember a day, or rather night, when I was marooned with four companions in the most appalling thunderstorm I have ever experienced. As second in command of the company it was my job to bring up the rear and make sure that there were no stragglers. Sometime towards dusk one of the men was taken ill with a severe attack of dysentery and for a time was quite unable to proceed. I had a corporal and my batman with me and we managed to get hold of the M.O. who was somewhere in the front. While he was attending to the casualty the rest of the column moved forward and in the pitch darkness we completely lost touch.

It was then that the thunderstorm caught us. It lasted several hours, in fact for the whole of the night. The flashes of lightning coming from a dozen places at once and running along the ground all round us in vivid blue streaks, accompanied by a continuous roll of thunder and a solid wall of rain, which turned the place into a quagmire, were really quite frightening. There was no question of our dismounting under those conditions and we crouched on our camels protecting our saddle bags as best we could. Somehow the casualty survived the ordeal, although he was so weak that he seemed to be in danger of falling off every minute. The camels were in an abject state of misery and remained standing the whole time in a tight circle with their heads facing inwards and moaning their discomfort to each other. The skies cleared some time after dawn and we were able to proceed, though we did not catch up with the rest of the column for several hours.

Meanwhile the cavalry were in full pursuit of the Turks and it was the role of Camel Corps to act as a screen between them and the infantry At night we would relieve the cavalry, when we could catch up with them, and give them much-needed rest and the opportunity to water their horses, always assuming that there was any water available.

One night I had to take my section to relieve a squadron of my old friends in Fayoum, the Lincolnshire Yeomanry. After they had drawn back we moved forward in search of a better position for the night and, rounding a corner, we came in sight of a solitary Turkish field gun, guarding a cleft between two small hills. It was only about 100 yards away and, in the vivid light of a full moon, we could clearly see the gun crew, one of whom was in the act of putting a shell into the breech, but there was no sound whatsoever except for the mournful sighs of a dying camel, which had come from God knows where (it was not one of ours). We took such cover as was available and waited to see what would happen next. Nothing happened at all and we gradually became aware of the immobility of the men behind the gun. After a few minutes we began to make our way cautiously forward, but there was still no sound or movement and, as we got closer, it became apparent that all of them were dead. They had been killed just where they stood, serving their gun to the last. Yet another instance of the courage of the ordinary Turkish soldier and his refusal to accept defeat. With one exception all of them were still standing at the gun and they gave the impression not so much of having been killed as having suddenly ceased to live. Their faces were unmarked and showed no trace of fear or even excitement. There was a field telephone close by and we traced the wire to the edge of a small prominence not more than fifty yards away, where we came across the body of a German officer, who had presumably been in command of this forlorn hope. I am afraid that there was nothing we could do except relieve him of his revolver and binoculars, which would be of no use to him any more.

There is no doubt that the impact of the cavalry played a tremendous part in the campaign and the one which finally broke the Turkish armies in the following year. I do not know exactly how many cavalry regiments there were in Palestine, but I do know that we used to talk in terms of 100,000 horses, which surely must have been an exaggeration. None the less it was one of the greatest, although certainly the last, of the cavalry wars and I think that, when their doom was finally sealed by the advent of modern weapons, with their terrific fire power, the last remaining romance went out of war for ever.

Not that the weapons which they had to face in Palestine could be described as anything but modern. It was more that the Turks simply did not have enough guns and particularly machine guns, to make the work of the cavalry virtually impossible. None the less some of the charges were carried out against almost impossible odds. Outstanding was that of the Warwickshire and Worcestershire Yeomanry against twelve guns which they captured, though at the expense of severe casualties. In the final stages the shells were bursting almost at the muzzles of the guns. Nearly all the Austrian gunners were killed at their posts and the Yeomanry swept on to attack the Turkish infantry who were in support, many of whom were killed or captured, while losing several machine guns into the bargain. Other charges in addition to those of the Australians and New Zealanders, were carried out by my own regiment the Berkshire Yeomanry and also the Dorsetshire Yeomanry and the Royal Bucks Hussars. It was on one of these occasions that Evelyn Rothschild and Neil Primrose were killed.

We passed through the battlefield a few hours later. There were many corpses lying around, and by an incredible and unhappy coincidence Sergeant-Major Guppy, who was a Dorset Yeoman, stumbled over one of the bodies only to discover it was that of his own brother.

Day after day the advance continued without a break on the heels of the retreating Turks, who although they put up tremendous resistance in countless engagements large and small, were becoming dispirited though never demoralised, under the tremendous pressure which was being exerted upon them. We always seemed to be just in or out of the line and I have a confused recollection of being constantly on the march for hours and even days on end, from which a few isolated instances stand out.

There was the capture of Yebna at dawn by our forward troops and tremendous excitement following a rumour that the redoubtable General von Falkenhayn himself had only escaped with minutes to spare.

There was also an occasion when we were held up by having to cross a steep wadi, where a Turkish mule train had been caught and destroyed. The place was littered with dead men and mules and overturned wagons through which the crossing had to be negotiated in almost total darkness. My batman, Neville, was riding in the rear of the column on my spare camel and he was sent up with a message for me. Unfortunately it was never delivered. In the general noise and confusion the camel bolted and went clean over the edge of the wadi, a drop of about fifteen feet, carrying my batman with him. That was the end of the camel, and for a time my batman as well.

A few days later there was the capture of a Jewish settlement called Richon le Zion. I do not recollect that we were received by the ' liberated ' Jews with any particular enthusiasm, although they seemed to be quite friendly. We had almost run out of food by then and, as the nearest supply column was miles in the rear and there was no question of requisitioning anything, we had to negotiate with our newly acquired friends for the purchase of sufficient food to keep us going. I seem to remember that they charged us a pretty stiff price and that for about two days we lived on a diet of semolina. This was just about enough to keep us from starvation until our rations arrived one evening and we were able to consume large quantities of bully beef and biscuit as we rode along into the night.

We took no part in the capture of Jerusalem itself and I shall not attempt to describe that feat of arms. We were assigned to a force consisting of one mounted and one infantry division, whose task was to secure the coastal region far to the north-west, while the bulk of the army was engaged in the Jerusalem sector. This deployment of his forces was afterwards referred to, at any rate by us, as Allenby's bluff. Admittedly we were very thin on the ground and, as far as we knew, there were no reserves behind us at all, so that if the Turks had counter-attacked in strength they must have broken through. But they seem to have been completely in the dark as to Allenby's real intentions and it may well be that they did regard the build up in the Jerusalem area as a screen for delivery of the main assault on the extreme right of their line as they faced towards the south and west.

On the 16th November Jaffa (or Joppa as it used to be called), the seaport of Jerusalem, was taken and a line was established in the vicinity of the river Auja. That was the furthest point which we reached and there as it happened we were to stay for several days. By this time our camels were in a pretty deplorable condition. Most of them had not been unsaddled for days and were suffering from severe sores, and even the most elementary grooming had been impossible since the attack on Beersheba nearly a month earlier. Even now very little could be done for them as we were constantly on the alert to move off at a moment's notice.

Our own front line consisted of three or four strong points on slightly higher ground than the surrounding plain with lateral and communicating trenches. Each of these was manned day and night in about half-company strength and I cannot say that they were particularly comfortable. The Turkish positions were not far away and although, despite many false alarms particularly at night, they did not launch an attack we were under intermittent shell fire the whole time and the trenches were continually being blown in and having to be restored. One of the casualties was Major Gregory, who was killed when a 5.9 shell fell on the strong point he was commanding. This was a sad loss to the Battalion as he was one of our best officers.

How long we remained in this sector of the line I cannot remember, but I do not think that it was until after the surrender of Jerusalem on the 9th December, that we were taken into reserve to rest and refit after a campaign which had lasted for exactly six weeks, for the greater part of which we had been constantly on the move. By now the condition of the camels, which had been bad enough before, was almost desperate. Some of them were almost too weak to stand up and most of them were past hope of curing. In many cases they had cavities on each side of their humps so deep that you could have buried a cricket ball in them. These cavities were, of course, septic and the raw flesh was alive with maggots. God only knows what these once-splendid animals must have suffered but they complained no more than usual, and stuck it out until they collapsed from exhaustion. Cruel though it may sound we had to saddle and load up the worst cases in order to preserve, if we could, those animals which had relatively minor sores by retaining them as spares. But in the event very few of them recovered. There was one pathetic march which I can vividly remember. Again I had to bring up the rear of the column, but this time with the veterinary instead of the medical officer. Camels were collapsing one after another and as there was no hope of ever getting them to their feet again their riders or loads, as the case might be, were being transferred to spares, many of which were to collapse in their turn before very long. As the column moved slowly forward we caught up with the fallen camels and put them out of their misery. How many were shot, I cannot say but looking back along the route we had passed, we could see an endless line of corpses fading into the distance. They had served us faithfully, poor devils, and we had become very attached to them, or at any rate to most of them.

In addition to sores and general weakness most of the camels had also developed a peculiarly virulent form of mange, but unfortunately they did not keep it to themselves. No doubt we were not in particularly good shape. Most of us were already suffering from septic sores particularly behind the knees and on our faces, which made shaving hell. However, we had done very little of this lately. Whether it was due to our poor condition or whether it would have happened anyway I have no idea but quite suddenly we were infected with the mange ourselves. Hardly anyone escaped. It was not too bad by day, but directly our bodies warmed up in our blankets at night (the weather had now become very cold and wet) the irritation became unbearable. It was impossible to sleep and the worst sufferers spent the whole night walking about. I doubt whether I have heard, before or since, such a variety of language. Our parlous condition was reported to the higher medical authorities and a special decontamination centre was established for our benefit. In the meantime we were put out of bounds, no other unit being allowed to approach us.

I cannot remember how long it was before we were passed as 'clean' again, but it must have been several days. During that time many of the remaining camels had to be destroyed or evacuated and towards the end of December we were ordered back to Rafa to recuperate and to receive a fresh supply of camels from the remount depot in the rear. There was no further outbreak of mange, but curiously enough I became infected again when I was in hospital in London in August of the following year.

Towards the end of December the Turks launched a heavy counter-attack with the object of retaking Jerusalem, but it failed to accomplish very much and they were finally driven back about fifteen miles to the north of the city. This brought an end to the winter campaign, which had lasted two months, during the first six weeks of which alone 25,000 casualties had been inflicted on the Turks in addition to the 12,000 captured. Volume 4 of *A Popular History of The Great War* edited by Sir J. A. Hammerton, records the following laconic sentence in Allenby's order of the day issued on the 15th December: ' In forty days many strong positions have been captured and the Force has advanced sixty miles on a thirty mile front.'

Incidentally it was widely believed that Allenby was held in the greatest admiration and respect by the ordinary Turkish soldier who thought that some supernatural and almost godlike figure had descended on them with the name of Allah Bey. They also had a saying, which was alleged to have come down through the centuries, that Jerusalem would fall when the waters of Egypt flowed into the city. It may well be, therefore, that the famous pipeline from Kantara had a significance for them which went far beyond the mere supply of water.

Not long after our arrival at Rafa we were all given in turn a few days' leave, and in due course Merlin Huth and I proceeded to Cairo where we put up at Shepheard's, which succeeded in maintaining the highest possible standard of living throughout the entire war, and it would be an understatement to say that we made the most of it, helped by the fact that our pay had been piling up for months and we had plenty of funds at our disposal. There were at least three bars, one of which was presided over by a gentleman called Hannibal, and was alleged to be the second largest in the world, the first being somewhere in Shanghai. There were also two enormous dining-rooms and the food was absolutely superb in its own right, and not simply by contrast with what we had been consuming during the last few months. We used to lunch every day in one or other of these, but if the weather was warm enough, which in early February was not always the case, we dined on the terrace overlooking the street. During the day we made various expeditions to places like Heluan, Heliopolis, near our old quarters at Abbassia, the beautiful Barrage Gardens, and, of course, Mena, where we inspected the Sphinx and climbed to the top of the Cheops Pyramid, only to be confronted by a very talkative character selling soft drinks at probably very exorbitant prices. It was not so bad going up, but when we started to descend it was quite a different matter and I seem to remember that, when we finally overcame our giddiness, we proceeded backwards lowering ourselves very gingerly from block to block. There was a story, though I cannot vouch for it, that just about that time three Australian soldiers, who had also been enjoying their leave, had a wager as to which of them could get to the bottom first, with fatal results as they were all killed. Certainly if you did have the misfortune to slip there was nothing to stop you until you reached the bottom.

Night life in Cairo during the First War was a pretty hectic and disreputable affair and I think the less I say about it the better. The trouble was that the more conventional forms of entertainment were denied to us. I cannot remember that anything was done to keep the troops amused and we were left very much to our own devices. There were one or two theatres and music halls, including the Kursaal, but we found the performances very dull and conducted in pretty well every language except English.

At the end of our leave we returned to Rafa where there was not a great deal to do except to prepare for the next operation whatever it might be and have an occasional jackal hunt. There were dozens of these creatures in the vicinity of the camp, and their howling at night almost drove us round the bend.

But there was one day which does stand out in my mind. It was decided to take advantage of the fact that practically the whole of the Camel Brigade, including the Australians and New Zealanders, was assembled at Rafa to hold a sort of gym-khana. I believe that there had been one or two of these before, but at a time when our company had been detached from the main body. It turned out to be rather a splendid affair. There were trotting races, galloping races, wrestling on camel-back, musical chairs, tug-of-wars (or should it be tugs-of-war?), sack races (not on camels), stunt riding, which included trotting and even galloping with the rider standing up behind the camel's hump, and prizes for such things as the best turned out section. So far as the latter was concerned, it is surprising what a little spit and polish can do even under desert conditions.

It was somewhere about this time that I received a letter from home saying that my surviving brother was going to be married shortly and suggesting that, as I had now been overseas for more than two years, it might be a good idea if I were to apply for a spell of home leave and attend the wedding. I thought that this was a good idea too. Unfortunately these things take a long time to arrange. My application was approved in succession by my commanding officer, the brigadier and the divisional commander. There remained apparently one more hurdle to surmount but it was not until several weeks later, when I had almost forgotten about it, that my application was returned with a note from the corps commander to the effect that, as he had just read an account of my brother's wedding in a paper which had come out from England, it was too late and he would have to deny himself the privilege of falling in with my suggestion!

Chapter Eleven

THE RAID ON AMMAN

THE RESUMPTION of hostilities after the winter lull, particularly in the Jordan Valley, led to the capture of Jericho on the 21st February, 1918, and by the end of the month the west bank of the Jordan had been completely cleared of the enemy from Jericho to the Dead Sea. In consequence the opportunity had now arisen to effect a crossing of the river and put into operation the plan which had been concocted between Allenby and Lawrence for a raid in force on the Hejaz railway by the British from the west acting in conjunction with the Arabs to the east. Although we knew nothing about it at the time the Camel Corps had been selected to play a leading part in this operation, and on the 10th March we were ordered to proceed to the Jordan Valley. I cannot remember very much about the first part of this journey, which was by easy stages, but in due course we found ourselves at King Solomon's Pools, a few miles south of the city and quite close to Bethlehem, where we stayed for several days.

By the 18th March we were on the move again, and in the early hours of the morning we topped a rise and saw Jerusalem spread before us. There was, I remember, a full moon and the city seemed to be bathed in silver, a beautiful sight which I shall never forget. Nor shall I forget the incredible silence as we passed through from one end to the other. There was not a soul to be seen, and the only sound came from our camels as they padded their way stealthily through the streets. Later on we passed the Mount of Olives and began our descent through the Judaean Hills towards the Jordan Valley and the Dead Sea. About half-way down we turned north from the road and camped for the night on the edge of a steep wadi. Next morning we were informed that a crossing of the Jordan had been effected and that we were to take part in a large-scale raid on Amman in Transjordania, with the object of blowing up sections of the railway, which ran through the town on its way from Damascus to Medina, and which was the chief line of communication for the Turks in the defence of Syria from Lawrence and his Arabs. The information that we should be starting on the following day, however, was incorrect as we had hardly wrapped ourselves in our blankets with the idea of getting a good night's sleep while we had the chance, when the order came through that we were to march at midnight.

By dawn we were in sight of Jericho and reaching the floor of the Jordan valley, the lowest place on earth (1300 feet below sea-level) and one of the hottest. During the summer months it is quite intolerable and, even though it was only March, the contrast between the conditions we encountered there and the cold and wet we had recently experienced on the higher ground was startling. All the morning was spent in traversing the wide expanse between the foothills and the river, but the ground was hard and level and we made such good time that by mid-day we had reached the Dead Sea, where we halted for a meal. The day was overcast and the water grey and uninviting with a ring of what looked like dirty soap-suds round the edge. I had bathed several times in the salt lakes at Mersa Matruh but they were clean and sparkling, whereas this vast expanse of water seemed to be just dirty and in fact as well as in name— dead. We crossed the river by a pontoon bridge which had been hastily erected by the sappers. The far side was pitted with shell craters and it was evident that the original crossing had been no easy task. The country now seemed to change, and for some reason we were diverted off the track and had to make our way for hours across a horrible swamp which meant very heavy going for the camels and considerably delayed our progress. There was an almost tropical variety of birds, some of which I had never come across before, including hundreds of storks which flew all round us with their pink legs trailing behind. And then it began to rain, a pitiless downpour, which was to last for forty-eight hours and turn the track through the Moabite Hills, or rather mountains, which we were now approaching, into a morass.

We had now been marching for some eighteen hours, except for the mid-day break by the Dead Sea, but this was only the beginning and after a two-hour halt to snatch a meal and a few minutes' sleep we were on our way again. It was a grim night but at least we kept on the move and, so far, the track was on comparatively level ground. However in the early hours of the morning we began the ascent and when dawn broke we must have reached an altitude of about 1000 feet and it was now that our troubles really began. As the track climbed up through the hills the sides grew steeper and steeper with sheer cliffs on one side and a precipice on the other. The camels struggled gamely but they were neither accustomed to such appalling conditions nor designed by nature to overcome them. The rain continued without a break, the track became worse and worse as the mud was churned up by the troops in front, and the camels at last began to falter as they struggled to keep their footing. Many of them did the splits with their legs splaying out in either direction, others slipped and went over the side of the ravine, and even if they were not fatally injured by the fall there was no way of getting them back again so that we had to climb down, remove their loads and shoot them where they lay. I think they must have welcomed being put out of their misery.

What with the rain and various traffic jams on the narrow track we did not seem to make much progress that day or the following night and it was pretty obvious that we were getting further and further behind schedule and the chances of surprising the Turks becoming more and more remote. Somewhere away on our left was the 60th (London) Division. A considerable part of Desert Mounted Corps, including various units of Australian and New Zealand Light Horse and most of the Camel Brigade, was also involved. Heavy fighting took place to the north and west in the region of Es Salt which was eventually occupied on the 25th March, and the Turkish or rather German High Command must by now have been alerted to the fact that the Hejaz railway and possibly Amman itself were in danger.

The weather got worse and worse and, with the prospect of yet another night without rest, the third in succession, the situation was far from encouraging. With darkness progress became slower and slower and was not helped by the fact that on at least one occasion we had to cross a small stream which could only be negotiated in single file. This created such interminable delay that it became difficult to avoid dropping off to sleep. I know that I dozed off myself for a few moments only to wake up and find the whole of my section, which was at that point riding four abreast, fast asleep, both camels and men, and that we could neither see nor hear anything in front of us. In the pitch darkness it was even impossible to see the track, such as it was, and the only thing to do was to leave it to the instinct of the camels to find their way. Some time later to my great relief we caught up with the column just as its rear files were crossing the stream. By dawn the rain had eased off a little but we were still several miles short of our immediate objective, which was a line of low hills to be used as a springboard for the impending attack on the Turkish positions. We still had to traverse some narrow defiles and it became necessary to dismount and lead the camels through as best we could. This is the only time I have seen men fall asleep as they walked, even in mid stride, and there were so many delays that we did not reach our positions until mid-day, some seventy-six hours after we had started out so hopefully. I remember that the junior officers tossed up as to who should be duty officer. I was one of the lucky ones and slept for seventeen hours without a break.

In the early morning we stood to arms and were briefed by the intelligence officer as regards the situation generally and the task which we were supposed to perform. The only thing I can remember was his insistence that the Turks had been completely taken by surprise (we found this rather difficult to believe) that they had no guns and that, if the attack was pressed home, they would not have time to bring up any artillery before our final objective had been reached. Considering that they were sitting astride the railway which was their principal line of communication, it seemed to us that this was highly improbable, and it very soon became apparent that it was also wholly inaccurate because the moment we left the cover of the hills (leaving our camels in the rear) the first salvoes arrived, and as we were already within range of rifle and machine gun fire from the Turkish trenches less than half a mile away on a completely open plain we began to sustain heavy casualties and, by the time we had got within 500 yards of the enemy, we became completely bogged down and unable to advance any further. The same situation was developing on our left and right and things began to look a little serious. We dug in for the night, which was relatively uneventful.

On the following morning our camels were brought up from the rear and placed in a small wadi just behind our position. Our company commander at the time was Captain Tredinnick, who had taken over a few weeks earlier from Julian Day, who had in turn succeeded Paterson, but was now at Battalion H.Q. Tredinnick was, I imagine, of Cornish extraction but was residing in South Africa at the outbreak of war. He was a

splendid soldier and had already been awarded the M.C.
Tredinnick was worried about the camels and decided to move
them further back which was very fortunate for all concerned
because, shortly after their departure, the wadi was heavily
shelled and undoubtedly most of the camels would have been
destroyed.

The Turks had now got the range of our positions all along
the line and it was impossilbe to make a move without attracting
a heavy burst of shell fire. In consequence we spent a frustrating
day and were not cheered up by the knowledge that the Turks
were being continually reinforced, whereas there was nothing
behind us at all. After dusk, however, we were able to make
some progress on our right and eventually established ourselves
in a trench of sorts about 100 yards from the Turkish positions.
The next morning was decidedly uncomfortable because in
addition to shell fire we were being sniped at continually from
the rear. It must be remembered that we were in hostile country
and it would be true to say that at least half the Arab population
in the villages were pro-Turkish and many of them in Turkish
pay. I have no doubt that the position would have been different
if the raid had looked like being a success, and in fact in the earlier
stages the villagers had turned out to welcome us. But they
had now discovered that far from being a general advance by
Allenby's army, which they had thought to be the case, this
was a relatively small operation and one which was already
beginning to founder. Inevitably, therefore, the Turks would
be reoccupying all the country through which we had passed
and it was not unnatural that enthusiasm for the Turkish cause,
whether real or feigned, was from now on to be the order of
the day.

On the rocky hillside to our right flank and behind us there
were a number of small caves large enough to hold perhaps a
couple of men, and as the sniping continued all that afternoon
we were able to pinpoint the little puffs of smoke which issued

from the mouth of each cave. Next morning came retribution. A couple of patrols were sent out and after climbing to the top of the hill some distance to the rear they were able to come down on the caves from above where they could not be seen and nonchalantly toss a Mills bomb inside. There was no more sniping. The following day the Turkish trenches were stormed by No. 9 Company, commanded by Captain Newsom, but at very heavy cost, Newsom himself and two of the other three officers being killed. Newsom had led the attack and was shot through the back at close range either by a German or an Austrian soldier, who had a moment before put his hands up and surrendered. Fighting was heavy and continuous and casualties began to grow alarmingly. These included Julian Day, who had come up to the front line, and who was severely wounded in the arm and shoulder.

Meanwhile, other forward units of the Camel Brigade and Light Horse had succeeded in reaching and blowing up several sections of the railway line, but not the station and tunnel complex at Amman, which was stoutly defended by the enemy, now in considerable force. That was virtually the end of the raid which had, I am afraid, accomplished very little. This was mainly due to the truly appalling weather in the early stages and the consequent delay and lack of surprise. I have seen it reported somewhere that during one of those awful nights on the mountain track the column had taken some twelve hours to cover two hundred yards.

Sometime during that uneasy night the order came to disengage, not quite so easy as it sounds with the enemy only a few yards away. We filed very quietly out of our positions and, as part of the rearguard, lay for hours at ten-yard intervals under cover of darkness while the wounded were being evacuated and the remainder of the column reorganised for the retreat back to the Jordan valley. It seems that the Turks were completely unaware of what was going on. Otherwise they would

surely have counter-attacked before we could reach the cover
of the hills and, even so, it was surprising that no attempt was
made to molest the column as it snaked its way through those
narrow defiles. It was rough going, and the wounded must
have suffered pretty badly, but there was no rain and we made
steady progress. What I chiefly remember was the expression
on the faces of the villagers, who spat in the dust as we passed
and made signs indicative of their keen desire to cut our throats
given the chance. In due course we reached the river at the
bridge of Ghoraniyeh (the troops called it by another name
which sounded very similar but meant something quite different!)
and crossed over to Jericho and the plain beyond. Here we had
our final adventure as we were caught in the open by a squadron
of German planes which proceeded to bomb us somewhat
casually. The attack was not pressed home, but we were extremely
frightened on account of the fact that several of the camels were
still laden with explosives which had been intended for the
demolition of the railway, and a direct hit on one of these
would have had highly unpleasant consequences for us all.

That was the end of this operation which is described in
Sir J. A. Hammerton's *History* as follows. His reference to
Arabs is, of course, to those fighting under Lawrence's command.

It appeared as though Allenby was beginning a new offensive
along the whole of the line. But this was not the fact. His main
purpose was a raid in some force on the Hejaz railway in conjunction
with the Arabs on the east. Allenby's operations had been designed
to clear his front in order that such a raid could be carried out.
They had succeeded, and he began to make his preparations. His
objective was Amman (Rabboth Amon), lying in a direct line
some thirty miles east of Jericho, or about twenty-five miles beyond
the Jordan, in the Bible land of Gilead.

Early in March the success of the Arabs in raiding the railway
and wiping out isolated Turkish posts had so irritated the German
command that a strong force had been dispatched south towards
Maan both to curb Arab activities and to protect that vital depot.

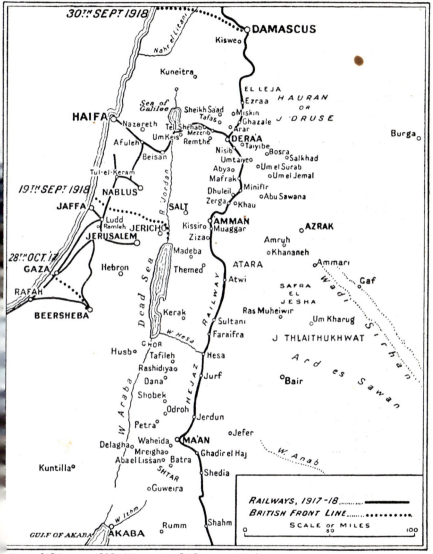

NOTE - "J." denotes JEBEL (Mountain)   "W." denotes WADI (Watercourse & Valley)

At Shobek the Arabs had been severely handled, but this reverse had not quenched their ardour or seriously limited their attacks on the railway. The Turkish force had therefore to remain at Maan. Allenby, by striking at Amman, was hoping to achieve one or more of three possible results. If the Turks remained at Maan his advance to Amman would be by so much the less resisted. He should, therefore, be able to seize the station and cut off the Turks in the south. If, however, they retired in order to resist his attack on Amman, then the Arabs should be able to occupy Maan. In any event, by careful co-operation, it might be possible for the two forces to make contact, and for the first time link up Allenby's main force with his right wing, as the Arab army eventually was named.

None of these expectations was wholly realised. The raid into Transjordania was begun on March 21 by sections of the 20th Corps assisted by part of the desert mounted corps. But the Turks made surprisingly strong resistance, and a whole day was spent in forcing the passage of the river. This delay was to prove serious eventually, but for the moment the troops pushed on. Difficult country and terrible weather further delayed the advance, and it was not until the evening of March 25th that Es Salt, to the north and west of Amman, was occupied. Everywhere the advance had been slow and painful, the Turks defending themselves with great courage. The railway north and south of Amman was finally reached by several patrols, and a number of culverts and several lengths of track were destroyed. But Amman itself proved invulnerable. In spite of heavy artillery bombardment and exemplary bravery among the British attacks, the Turks beat off attack after attack. By April 1 it was clear the raid had failed. Enemy reinforcements were pouring in from the north, seriously threatening the communications of the raiding force. Retreat was imperative, so Major-General Shea, in command of the operations, ordered the withdrawal. By April 2 the British troops were back in the Jordan valley.

The disappointment was felt keenly by the British, and the Turks were correspondingly elated. In particular it was a happy augury for von Sanders. But the repulse at Amman was not a serious reverse, and although the raid achieved little, the Turks had no cause for jubilation. Weather, difficult country, and the twenty-four hours' delay in crossing the Jordan had been the main factors in the failure. But great credit must be given to a German battalion of the Asia Corps, which fought with admirable determination. By its steadiness, bravery and discipline it did much to hold up the British advance, and provided a strong backbone on which the heterogeneous Turkish forces rallied.

In other words we got a bloody nose!

Chapter Twelve

THE JORDAN VALLEY
—MUSELLABEH

SHORTLY AFTER our return to the valley Tredinnick was appointed adjutant to the battalion, and I was given command of the company which I retained until my departure from the scene a month later. I do not know whether it was exceptional or not but by mid-April the place was becoming like a furnace. It was not only that on most days the temperature rose to nearly 100°, but at that low altitude the air such as it was seemed to be stagnant and unwholesome. Conditions were not improved by the fact that, when at dawn the mosquitoes desisted from their attacks, the flies took over, and if there were thousands of mosquitoes there were millions of flies. At meal-times their attentions became unbearable and it was impossible to raise a mug to one's lips without having to force one's way through the black mass clustered on the brim. On one occasion I gave up the unequal struggle and, instead of drinking, banged my mug hard on the table so that all the flies fell into the tea and were drowned, and I counted more than 200 corpses. It said a lot for the many injections we had received that we did not have an epidemic of typhoid. Some of the mosquitoes were of a particularly unpleasant kind, and for those men unfortunate enough to become infected produced a malignant form of malaria. Curiously enough I did not develop the disease until two months after I left the valley, and even then in a form which is euphemistically described as benign.

A few miles to the north of Jericho there is a hill called Musel-labeh. It is on the Judaean side of the valley and, rising sharply from the plain, it is quite a feature of the landscape. I do not know when it was first occupied by our troops, which were extended from the hills on the west to the Jordan river on the east, but there was no doubt as to its being the strongest point in the line, and with the prospect of a counter-attack by the Turks it was vital that we should retain it. Although I have referred to the Judaean hills, and the Moabite hills on the other side, it must be remembered that some of these rose to as much as 3000 feet above sea-level, and therefore nearly 4500 feet above the level of the valley. This gave the impression that we were surrounded on both sides by mountains rather than hills, and they certainly created a formidable rampart.

Despite its importance, and the fact that so long as it remained in our hands the Turks would be unable to take full advantage of any gains they might make on the lower ground, Musellabeh could not be held in more than company strength owing to the restricted area on the top of the hill. I remember it well because early in April I was ordered with my company to take over command of the hill from an infantry unit which had been occupying the place for some time. It was certainly an odd sort of place. Company H.Q. was set up in a small cave formed by an overhang of rock some forty or fifty yards to the rear of the trenches which lipped the northern edge of the hill but were so shallow, because the hill itself was not much more than a solid mass of rock, that they gave very little cover anyway.

From these there was a splendid field of vision in some directions, but it did not include the ground immediately below the hill, which owing to its steep sides, was completely hidden from the defenders. Moreover, the enemy had several batteries, mostly German, hidden in the hills to the west, and although we could not see them we knew very well that they could see us. There were also various shallow wadis leading from the hills which would give the enemy infantry an easy avenue of approach under cover of darkness to the broken ground below the hill, where they would be out of sight from above. Finally there was another hill in front of Musellabeh, which effectually screened any preparations for an attack which might be going on behind. It will be seen, therefore, that although in one sense Musellabeh was undoubtedly a very strong point in defence, in another it was highly vulnerable.

We remained on Musellabeh for several days doing what we could to strengthen the defences, and although it was perfectly obvious that an attack was imminent we had a fairly peaceful time, apart from sporadic bursts of shell fire which were mostly on the lower ground and did little damage.

In due course we were relieved by one of the Australian companies and I handed over to its commanding officer, Captain Mills, who had already been awarded the M.C. and was to get another very well-deserved one a few days later. It was either on that or the next night that I was woken up from our position in the rear by the noise of a furious bombardment, and to see the whole of Musellabeh literally exploding into flame. It did not seem possible that anybody could still be alive on that rocky exposed little plateau. As it happened, however, the Australians did not sustain heavy casualties on that occasion and, although the bombardment was followed by an infantry attack, this was broken up by our artillery before it could be pressed home and the enemy retired in some confusion. The main attack came two days later and is vividly described by Oliver Hogue in his book *The Cameliers*, which I have already mentioned.

The attack, as he described it, was again preceded by a violent bombardment under cover of which, accompanied by concentrated fire from German machine gunners posted on the hill to which I have referred, the enemy were able to make their way into the 'dead' ground below Musellabeh where they were out of sight, and from where they launched a concerted frontal attack up the steep side of the hill on the Australian positions. But if the enemy were outside the vision of the Australians, although only a few yards separated them, the reverse was also the case and the battle developed into a bombing duel with the Turks hurling up their grenades from below and the Australians 'lobbing theirs gently on the brow of the hill in such a way that the momentum caused them to roll nicely on to the Turks before exploding'.

Still it was touch and go and in places the Australians ran out of bombs and were reduced to heaving large boulders over the brow of the hill on to the hidden enemy. Eventually, however, the attacks which had been coming from the sides as well as from the front, began to fade away and the Australians remained 'the undisputed masters of Musellabeh'. Not, however, before they had sustained heavy casualties, including all the officers on the hill, one of whom was killed and the rest wounded. That was the last attempt by the enemy to capture Musellabeh and, although for several more days the Australian defenders were subjected to heavy shell fire, the fighting was virtually over. It was indeed a triumph and Allenby came in person to congratulate them on their performance. Many decorations were awarded, including Military Crosses to Mills and two of his officers, and Allenby in an order of the day proclaimed that, to commemorate the defence, Musellabeh would in future be known as 'The Camel's Hump'.

Chapter Thirteen

THE BRIDGE

THE REST of April passed peacefully enough apart from the heat, flies and mosquitoes and an occasional exchange of shell fire between the opposing batteries.

There was quite a variety of game in the valley and I remember borrowing a gun from somewhere one evening and having a little expedition on my own during which I shot three different species of partridge, which made a welcome addition to the larder.

However, just before midnight on the 30th April, I was woken by the Intelligence officer (the same gentleman who had told us before the attack on Amman that the Turks had no guns) who informed me that our troops on the other side of the river were attacking the Turkish positions at dawn and that my company had been ordered to go forward on the west bank and destroy a bridge which was a vital link in the Turkish lateral line of communication. The unit which held our front line in this sector was to stay put and we were to pass through it on our way to the bridge. Two guides from the unit in question would be reporting to me at 3 a.m. and would conduct us to the place from which we were to make the attack at dawn so as to coincide with the advance on the other side. A battery of guns was also moving into position so as to give us covering fire.

It did not seem to me that I was being given a great deal of time to mount this operation. In fact the chance of making a preliminary reconnaissance of the ground would have been negligible anyway, and what chance there was disappeared entirely when the guides, who reported punctually enough, proceeded to lose their way, with the result that we arrived at the front line an hour late. I hurriedly reported to the colonel in charge of the sector, who did not seem to know much more about the terrain than I did myself. He handed over to me several boxes of Mills bombs, which I afterwards discovered had not been primed and were quite useless, and told me that the Turks were in considerable strength and that for the last week his men had been having a very bad time. Nobody seemed to know exactly where the bridge was and what with this, the lateness of the hour (dawn was already breaking) and the fact that I had only about seventy men under my command, I began to be a little depressed and was not made any happier by the news that our supporting guns had not arrived. It seems that their guides had also lost their way!

I went forward to make some sort of a reconnaissance leaving Merlin Huth to bring up the company. Unfortunately there was little to see except that for the first few hundred yards we should be in broken ground where we should be invisible from the enemy, after which on our main front we would have to emerge on a flat plain about 600 yards short of the Turkish trenches. On our right flank bordering the river the broken ground continued and I ordered Huth to take a section and probe this as far as he could. It was now broad daylight and as the supporting barrage, which we had been promised, failed to materialise our situation could hardly be described as reassuring.

Directly we emerged on to the plain we came under heavy rifle and machine gun fire and began to sustain casualties, which we could not afford if we were going to do anything about that wretched bridge which we had not yet seen, and in fact never did see. I do not know how long we continued to make any progress but as the Turkish fire increased, not only from the front but the flanks as well, supported by shrapnel from their guns, it became obvious that we could not go on much longer. I sent a runner to Huth on my right to tell him to hold his ground as long as he could, and from his position in the broken ground help to cover our withdrawal in the centre, and another runner to my two Lewis gun teams on our left with instructions to do the same. The first runner was killed before he could deliver his message and in the event Huth and his remaining men only got away by the skin of their teeth. The Lewis gunners put up a great performance and continued firing up to the last possible moment. By now we were in a pretty bad way in the centre, and all the men in my leading section had been killed or wounded, I managed to work out some sort of orders for our general withdrawal by stages which were very well carried out. Unfortunately it was at this crucial moment that I was knocked head over heels like a rabbit by a bullet which passed through my left forearm fracturing both the bones. It made a bit of a mess but I was helped by two of my men who converged on me from different directions and refused to leave my side until they had brought me safely back to cover. Meanwhile the Turks were scrambling from their trenches in the hope, I suppose, of delivering the *coup de grâce*, but our guns had arrived at last and, although they had not been able to help us in our advance, they put down a very effective barrage to cover our retreat.

So ended an operation which I do not think could ever have succeeded, even if we had managed to get within bombing distance of the Turks, bearing in mind that the bombs we were carrying were nothing more than useless lumps of metal. It was a sad day. A third of the company had been killed or wounded and to make matters worse several of the latter had been taken prisoner.

I had supposed that our failure to carry out our task would not go down very well with my superiors and was more than relieved when I received in hospital a few days later a very kind and encouraging letter from Major Buxton, now commanding the Battalion, which showed that my fears on this score were quite unfounded.

After getting back to the front line about two hours after leaving it we rested for some time but, as the day wore on, it was decided that the walking wounded should make their way to the nearest dressing station which was some distance to the rear, and leaving Huth in command of the company, I accompanied them. It was a slow and painful journey, but eventually we arrived at a cluster of bell tents, which were occupied by an Australian medical unit which treated us with the utmost kindness and efficiency. In those days it was usual for the anti-tetanus injection to be made in the stomach, and I remember the M.O. standing over the bed on which I was lying and struggling to reach me with his needle through a horde of buzzing flies, which, as I have already described, presented an almost insoluble problem in the Jordan valley, even under conditions which were made as hygienic as possible. Quite rightly no attempt was made to dress our wounds and in fact it was not until three days later that I had my bandages removed for the first time. The next stage in my journey was by cacolet and I remember that I occupied one of the stretchers and my sergeant-major the other. At the next dressing station we became separated and my last link with the men with whom I had been serving for the last two years was severed, apart from those who were able to come and see me in hospital in Alexandria when they were on leave.

From there I proceeded on a led horse and some time in the evening arrived at the main casualty clearing station where I remained for some time before joining up with a convoy of motor ambulances which took us to a hospital in Jerusalem where we arrived about midnight. My particular ambulance had no lights had the driver and only the tail-lights of the one in front and the head-lights of the one behind to guide him on that precipitous and winding road so that it was a rather hair-raising experience.

It would be convenient here to refer to Hammerton's description of the operations which had been proceeding on the other side of the Jordan, and I fear that these too had been a flop. The idea had been to destroy the enemy force at Shunet Nimri, a few miles east of the bridge of Ghoraniyeh, and reoccupy Es Salt pending relief by Lawrence and his Arabs. The 60th Division was again involved, with the assistance of a mounted division. All went well at first and the 60th succeeded in occupying the outskirts of Shunet Nimri, but found themselves unable to proceed any further in the face of stubborn opposition. The mounted troops moved northwards round the right of the Shunet Nimri position and succeeded in capturing Es Salt, leaving an Australian brigade to protect their left flank, but in the early morning of the 1st May this brigade was heavily attacked by a Turkish cavalry division supported by infantry, which had crossed during the night from the west bank of the Jordan over a bridge, which I fear may have been the one I had been supposed to destroy and was at that moment struggling to reach. The Australians and in turn the troops at Es Salt and Shunet Nimri were forced to withdraw and in fact only got away with the utmost difficulty, several of their guns and part of their transport having to be abandoned in the process. Thus, although by the 4th May they managed to re-cross the Jordan with very little loss, there can be no disputing the fact that the raid, if you can call it that, was as much a reverse as the earlier one on Amman.

I only spent one night in Jerusalem and on the following day was conveyed to the railway station, from where several of us accomplished the next part of the journey in a closed wagon, the floor of which was covered in straw. Incidentally it is curious to reflect that, although during the last six weeks I had passed twice through Jerusalem and spent one night there, I had scarcely seen the place or, so far as I can remember, any of its inhabitants. In fact I never really did see it until May, 1967, a few weeks before the Six Day Arab-Israel War, when my wife and I paid a visit to Jerusalem, Jericho and Amman. It all seemed peaceful enough then and there was no sign of any impending hostilities.

The second and third nights we spent at successive field hospitals and it was on the latter occasion that my bandages were removed for the first time and my wound dressed. By then I was beginning to feel decidedly the worse for wear. However, we were now to experience the comparative comfort of a hospital train and we spent the fourth night in another field hospital at Kantara on the canal. On the following morning we crossed the canal and travelled on another hospital train to Alexandria, which we reached late that night, and were finally accommodated in a large base hospital after a journey which had lasted five days since I and my companions, many of whom came from other units, had become casualties. I must confess that after the wonderful treatment we had received all the way down the line we found the base hospital a somewhat impersonal and comfortless place. We were told that, as it was so late, our wounds would not be examined until the morning. As, however, mine had obviously turned septic I insisted on having immediate attention, and after removing the bandages the nurse hurriedly fetched a doctor who did whatever was necessary.

I remained in that hospital for three months which seemed to be very long ones. There was nothing to do and I do not remember that we were ever provided with any sort of entertainment. Some time during the first month we were enlivened by a visit from Allenby on one of his tours of inspection. He spent a long time in the ward and insisted on talking to us all and enquiring how we came to be there, what units we came from and in what particular section of the line we had been serving. He gave the appearance, and I am sure it was perfectly genuine, of really being interested in our various experiences.

He was a great soldier and a great man, and I think that we were all of us proud to have served under his command.

Unfortunately my arm refused to heal and, after I had been in hospital a month, it was opened up and some bone splinters which were the cause of the trouble were removed. One look at it, however, a few days after the operation was sufficient to convince the medical board that I should return to England on the next available ship, but unfortunately I chose this moment to fall ill with a very high fever. The obvious explanation was malaria but blood tests proved to be negative and it was decided that I was probably suffering from a severe attack of infective jaundice (I had never heard of such a thing) and would have to be isolated. I certainly looked incredibly yellow! A final decision was to be made next day by which time, however, my temperature had dropped to normal and, as I steadily continued to improve, I was allowed to stay in the ward under observation for the next week. I recovered completely but on the day before I was finally cleared the hospital ship sailed and the next one was not due for another month. It was two and a half years since I had left home and I was almost in despair. Moreover, as became evident soon after I eventually got back to England, it had been malaria all the time!

Chapter Fourteen

THE HEJAZ ASSAULT COLUMN

SOME TIME after the raid on Amman and the conclusion of the
operations in the Jordan valley which I have already described
Allenby came to the decision that the main body of the Camel
Corps should be disbanded. Camels were hardly suitable for
the sort of country over which any future advance would have
to be made and in any case he was in need of the additional
cavalry which the Camel Corps could supply. Although,
however, most of them were to go to stiffen the newly arrived
Indian cavalry brigades Allenby acceded to Lawrence's request
that a detachment of 300 men and 400 camels should be loaned
to him for operations against and beyond the Hejaz railway.
This was placed under the command of Major Buxton, who
was later promoted to Lieutenant-Colonel and awarded the
D.S.O. Laurence Moore went in charge of signals and I propose
to give an account of the operations which followed in his
own words.

We rode back through Jericho and Jerusalem, over the Judaean
hills, through Beersheba and across the Sinai desert to our base at
Ismailia on the Suez Canal, where we were to refit and change our
camels. The remaining 3000 camels were to be presented to
Lawrence and we thought we might as well select the best for
ourselves before we followed them.

We picked up extra ammunition and large supplies of explosives
to take with us and trekked over the south eastern lobe of the
Sinai Peninsula through Nakhl to Akaba. Lawrence came out to
meet us and rode the last day in our company during which he

warned us of the kind of greeting we might expect on our arrival. In spite of his warning, however, we were not quite prepared for what actually happened. There were thousands of Arabs milling around on foot, on horse, on camel, all of them blazing away with their rifles into the air in what Lawrence called a *feu de joie*, but which we thought a shocking waste of small arms ammunition brought across the Mediterranean at considerable risk by the Royal and Merchant Navies. Several bullets came uncomfortably close and, when we eventually halted, some of the men found bullet holes clean through their solar topees. This probably was one of the reasons why some of the British troops in that sector subsequently discarded them in favour of a khaki Arab headcloth which presented no target above the skull. Later on we went to swim in the sea, the Gulf of Akaba, while the Arabs sat on the shore taking pot shots in our direction with the bullets pinging and splashing all round our heads. When we mildly remonstrated they said that they were protecting us by driving off the sharks!

Lawrence gave us another talk after our arrival and explained that the Arabs of Arabia were quite different—more independent and tougher—from those in Egypt or the Western Desert and he begged us, whatever happened and however provocative or aggressive they might appear to be, not to show any signs of annoyance or fear but rather to 'turn the other cheek'. He asked us this, he said, not only because of our western understanding but because they were so many and we were so few. That night, as usual, we 'formed square' a useful formation, with the camels on the outside, saddlery on the inside and men inside that. The camels kept off the cold wind of the desert and would help protect us against a sudden sandstorm or the odd stray bullet. There were no enemy within 100 miles so we lighted up our fires, and there were many because the Camel Corps always messed in groups of four. Meanwhile the bullets continued to whistle over our heads as the Arabs capered around and cracked away with their rifles. If anybody interferes with the tea-making process of the British soldier there is usually a pretty violent reaction and, when eventually one or two of the tea billies were punctured by the flying bullets, a couple of our men picked up some Mills bombs and were on the point of sailing into the Arabs when Lawrence arrived on the scene and restrained them. He stood in the middle of the square, flung back his *aba*, showing his white undergarment and, illumined by

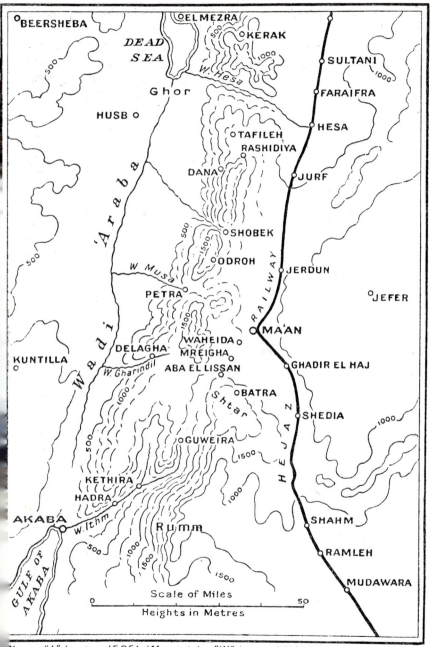

NOTE _ "J." denotes JEBEL (Mountain)   "W." denotes WADI (Watercourse & Valley)

the countless fires, raised his hand. Immediately the firing ceased, the hubbub died down and we had a peaceful night.

It was either that night or the next that Lawrence asked Major Buxton for permission to address the men and explain why he had sent for us, a most unusual experience during World War One, when it was only on very rare occasions for a commander to take the troops into his confidence. The Arabs, he said, would sit on the hilltops taking pot shots at the enemy but they would not tackle strongly fortified positions. Also they would never attack in the dark and, unless we assaulted some of the Turkish positions during the hours of darkness, we would have no chance of surprising them. He had told the Arabs that we were the bravest soldiers in the world and he begged us to live up to the reputation he had built up for us because, he went on to say, if we did fail in any of our attacks the Arabs might well interfere with our retreat. They would certainly snipe at us from the hilltops and deny us the use of their wells.

He also begged us, as soon as we captured a Turkish position, to clear out and leave it to the Arabs whose principal interest in war was loot. We rather chuckled at this because some of the Camel Corps lads were pretty quick and handy with loot themselves, particularly if there was any liquor around, which only occurred if there had been some German officers in the position. We were also on the look out for certain articles of equipment such as Zeiss or Goertz binoculars and prismatic compasses, Luger automatic pistols, Mauser telescopic sights and a rather natty line in bivouac sheets, which were very popular with the Turkish officers. The Arabs on the other hand looked for, in descending order, horses—preferably mares—camels, sheep or goats and, failing any of these, women. I do not remember that we were ever able to provide them with any of the latter!

The following day we went out to do our first job for Lawrence, which was to capture and destroy the Turkish fortress at Mudowra, roughly half way along the railway line between Damascus and Medina, and a watering point for the locomotives. If we could destroy the pumping station we could put the line out of action for a very long time. We marched out of Akaba with Lawrence at the head of the column and his bodyguard, forty hand picked Arabs from different tribes, whom we naturally called ' The Forty Thieves'. They were most handsomely caparisoned with fancy waistcoats, stripes and polka dots, their hair perfumed, greased and ringleted, quite desperate characters really but faithful in their service to Lawrence.

I rode with them most of the way until we reached the watering place at Rumm. The spring was in reality nothing more than a trickle of water percolating through a layer of porous or fissured rock on a shelf about 300 feet up an almost vertical cliff, and all the water had to be collected up there and lowered to the ground in canvas buckets. It took us more than thirty hours to water our 400 camels. Meanwhile Lawrence went off for two days with Buxton and some of the other officers including my company commander, Captain Joe Lyall, all dressed up as Arabs but with rifles under their cloaks, to reconnoitre the position of Mudowra and, while they were away, some trouble arose at the spring. Some of our men called down and asked me to come up and help with some Arabs who were chivvying them off the shelf with the risk of a horrible fall. I clambered up and asked the Arabs what it was all about and announced that I was in the service of the Sherif Feisal. They took one look at me and said ' Min Int ' (Who are you?). In perfect truth I replied ' Ismi Hurrence ' (My name is Laurence) and when I saw their look of incredulity I quickly added ' Ahu Hurrence ' (the brother of Lawrence). At least, I thought, I am his brother in arms! None of them apparently had ever seen Lawrence but eventually they found a little chap at the back who claimed that he had, and they dragged him forward and confronted him with me. He took one look and announced ' Yea, the same mad blue eyes, the same red face. Verily this is the brother of Lawrence '. There was immediate peace, and it was amazing to us that the very mention of Lawrence's name to a crowd of Arabs, who had never seen him but only heard of his reputation, could produce such a moving effect. It transpired later that they were a sub-clan of the Amran/Howeitat, the local tribe to whose Sheikh we had paid 100 golden sovereigns for permission to water from the ' spring '.

Lawrence warned us to drink deeply of the waters of Rumm because, if we failed at Mudowra, the Howeitat would forbid us the use of their water on the way back. So it was up to us to succeed as this was the only hope of our next drink. Fortunately the tactical plan, which had been drawn up by Buxton, worked perfectly and the operation was a complete success. We approached the strongly fortified positions from the rear in complete darkness during the early hours of the morning and, when daylight came, we had captured nearly the whole position except for one redoubt, a natural hill surmounted by stone sangars. Protected as it was by one or two field guns and several heavy machine guns it was a bit too tough for our small raiding party, which had been sent out to make a diversion from the front, to take by assault. However, Lawrence provided for this. When the light was good a couple of planes of the Hejaz flight came over and I had the job of controlling what must have been one of the first ever ground-to-air-controlled bombardments. We had no radio so the planes spoke to me in Morse by Klaxon horn, and I was able to tell them where I was by smoke bomb and put out letter signals by prearranged code. After the planes had each dropped, from almost ground level, a couple of sixty pound bombs on to the stony Northern Redoubt, the Turks came streaming out, waving any dirty rag that could serve as a white flag, and I gave the planes the signal ' Cease Fire '.

Our prisoners outnumbered ourselves and, as we obviously could not spare anyone to escort them, they had to be taken back to Akaba by the Arabs. Lawrence knew perfectly well that, if he paid the Bedouin in advance, they would march the prisoners behind the nearest hill and shoot the lot, so they were paid at the rate of one pound in gold for each prisoner who arrived at Akaba alive, which they all did. The Turkish officers strongly objected to this arrangement, but they had to put up with it.

The nearest Field Ambulance was back in Akaba, and our wounded had a most gruelling journey. Captain Lyall, who was badly hit by what was almost the last shot in the action as he was conducting his prisoners from the Southern Redoubt over the 300 yards or so of open ground to the station buildings, told me later that, after some three days of painful progress in the blistering heat, they were all in a bad way, but a plane came over and dropped a note telling them to camp where they were until R.A.F. trucks arrived to pick them up and take them on to a rough landing ground, where they arrived about midnight. Next day they were carried to Akaba, but some of them did not survive. One of those who died just as he reached the hospital was my friend Corporal Jack Freeman, who was posthumously awarded the D.C.M.

Meanwhile, after handing over the captured rifles and S.A.A. to the Arabs, we threw the field guns with their ammunition into the

well and blew up the whole lot, together with the pumps and other
machinery, generally making a complete wreck of the place.
One of our demolition experts was Bimbashi Peake of the Egyptian
Army, later to become famous as Peake Pasha, founder of the
Jordanian Arab Legion. (*Author's note.* Peake Pasha (Lt.-Col.
Frederick Gerard Peake) died in March 1970.) Afterwards we
rode up the railway line for several miles, blowing up every bridge
and culvert on the way. (In point of fact, although the well at
Mudowra, which later became a fort of the Arab Legion under
Glubb Pasha, must have been reconstructed, and parts of the line
further to the north have certainly been repaired, I do not believe
that a single train has passed through Mudowra since that day, and
even the Arab historians agree that the line was not completely
severed until by the Imperial Camel Corps in August, 1918.) And
then at last, as the dusk came, we turned towards the east and
melted into the desert night and I must confess that it was quite a
thrill, as our camels daintily picked their way over the metals, to
realise that we were indeed a British force at large behind the
enemy lines.

We rode about 100 miles east, then about the same distance to
the north, and finally we turned west towards the railway again.
To avoid the Turkish or rather German planes we moved only
during the hours of darkness. In the daylight and moonlight we
lay up in the cracks and crannies of the various wadis. We could
move only at the walk, about three miles per hour, because of the
enormous loads of ammunition and explosives, which we had to
carry with us, so it all took a long, long time.

During one of the midday halts Arthur Collins (who was respons-
ible for keeping track of the gold we paid out to the Arabs for
water, guides or other services) and I were seeking what shelter
we could find from the glaring sun under an army blanket strung
across some of my signal flags, when we suddenly observed that an
Arab, armed with a rifle, was apparently stalking Lawrence, who
was himself sheltering under a similar contraption a few yards
away and reading as usual. As we caught sight of him the Arab
flattened out to take aim and I grabbed for a gun but he beat me
to it and fired. The bullet sent up a flurry of sand and feathers
about a yard from where Lawrence lay and the Arab calmly walked
forward and picked up the shattered remnants of a small sand
grouse, which he had blown to bits, and carried them away.

Lawrence merely raised his head for a moment and then resumed his reading. We agreed that it was a most fortunate occurrence that the Arab, who turned out to be one of Lawrence's bodyguard, had beaten me to the draw. Otherwise there might have been severe repercussions leading to an international, or rather inter-allied crisis!

One night we were halted and told we were just east of the railway at Kissela, five miles south of Amman, where lay our second objective, the very same viaduct and tunnel complex against which we had failed, from the other or western side, the previous March. Lawrence had persuaded Allenby that, where a whole division and more had a few months earlier failed in a frontal attack, a handful of determined men properly equipped, each one an expert in his own job, might succeed if they could attack by the back door. And here we were, within three miles of our former position on the other side of the railway line, although we had ridden rather more than 1000 miles to get there.

In the result, however, we were to be disappointed. By now, owing to casualties and other reasons, our effective strength had been reduced to less than 200 and reconnaisance established the fact that a Turkish cavalry regiment was actually stabling its horses in the very viaduct we were to blow up, so that although we were confident that we could overcome them Lawrence and Buxton decided that we would be unable to do so in sufficient time before heavy reinforcements arrived from Amman, and with deep regret the whole affair was called off. So once again Amman defeated us.

Lawrence then announced that he had orders from Allenby that, in the event of our being unable to demolish the viaduct, we were to make the Turks aware of our presence and give them the impression that we were a much larger force than in fact we were. This we did in many ways. First of all every man opened three or four tins of bully beef, which was the only food that ever arrived with the caravans, and destroyed or burnt the contents leaving the tins lying about. This was no particular sacrifice because we found it impossible to eat it in that savage heat and the Arabs never ate it anyway. We lighted fires, making a great deal of noise in the process, the light cars were ordered to criss-cross the desert in every direction to make a lot of tracks, and we dropped the camel dung, which we carried for our fires, to add to our camels' normal droppings and give the impression that we had with us three or four times the number of camels which would be required by a relatively small raiding party such as in fact we were. My own contribution was to scribble some meaningless rubbish on army signal forms and leave them scattered around. And then once more we melted away into the eastern desert, with the Turkish cavalry probing cautiously behind us. It is worth mentioning here that the Arabs very rarely fed their camels on hard corn so that their droppings were easily distinguished from those of our own camels, which contained grains of *dhurra*, a kind of millet. Since the whole object was to deceive the enemy into thinking that the Camel Corps was present in considerable strength we had to confine ourselves to the latter.

Some days later, after dividing into small groups scattered over a wide front, so that any aerial reconnaisance by the enemy would find it difficult to calculate our numbers, we arrived at the oasis and fort of Azrak, where we bathed in the springs, and here there occurred the sort of unfortunate incident which had always seemed just around the corner, so to speak, but had never actually happened until now. While we were watering, Lieutenant Rowan, of our No. 7 Company, momentarily forgot the advice given by Lawrence to ' turn the other cheek '. The Arabs as usual were chivvying our fellows off the watering point. I was close to Rowan at the time and saw and heard him raise his sjambok and curse them in what we used to call Cairo Arabic. The Arabs muttered and slunk away and a little later there was a shot from the rim of the crowd which killed him instantly. Lawrence referred to this incident in *Seven Pillars of Wisdom* and said that it was an accident caused by an Arab, who had dropped his rifle, while shooting fish in the fort pool, but I cannot help the feeling, which is shared by my comrades who were there at the time, that it would have been virtually impossible for a bullet from a dropped rifle to have killed a man standing on a plinth with his head above the rest of the crowd some fifty feet away, and that the incident may have had a more sinister explanation, which might have been omitted for reasons of political expediency!

(*Author's note*. Rowan was the intelligence officer at Battalion H.Q. who had told us the previous March, mistakenly as it turned out, that the Turks had no artillery at Amman, and had a few weeks later woken me in the early hours of the morning with orders from H.Q. to take my company down to the Jordan and destroy the bridge which formed part of the Turkish lateral lines of communication. Some time after I had returned to England I heard, though I have forgotten from what source, that Rowan had been killed by an Arab. Nothing was said about an accident.)

In due course we returned to the railway and engaged in various diversions and demolitions in the vicinity of Maan, which was held by a full division of Turkish troops, until at last we arrived at the Headquarters of the Sherif Feisal (later King of Iraq) at Abu el Lissan, where he reviewed us with his G.O.C. Jafar Pasha, who had been captured by the Dorset Yeomanry during a charge against the Senussi, and had subsequently been released after the Arab revolt to take command of their ' regular ' army. We understood that we were to receive a Hejaz medal, but it never materialised!

After we left Abu el Lissan we made an expedition, again and for the last time led by Lawrence, to the famous Gorge at Petra and returned from there to one of our bases at Beersheba, where our camels had a long awaited graze and rest, the first for many months.

So ended our operations in the Hejaz though our second-in-command, Lord Winterton, remained behind with Feisal and Lawrence and he accompanied the latter on the subsequent Arab march to Deraa and the capture of Damascus, as related in *Seven Pillars of Wisdom* which, among its many illustrations includes drawings of Lord Winterton and Colonel Buxton. Lord Winterton was a very tall man and his height was accentuated by his extreme leanness. He was also a very brave one. There was an occasion when he was standing up on a parapet observing with his glasses and in full view of the enemy. Bullets were spattering all round and the men behind him were imploring him to come down or he would get pipped to which he replied ' They'll not pip me, I'm too d - - - - d thin '!

A few days later Allenby launched his final and overwhelming offensive which was to put the Turks out of the war and cause them to sue for an armistice, and it is no exaggeration to say that he was helped by the fact that, because the Turks were misled into thinking that the whole of the Imperial Camel Brigade was present in the Hejaz, they substantially reinforced the Amman-Maan area, thus weakening their main front in Palestine.

It would, I think be helpful if I were to supplement the above account with some further details I have received from Laurence Moore, Captain Lyall and others, commencing with the text of the relevant Operations Order issued by the General Staff, Hejaz Operations, Savoy Hotel, Cairo, on the 16th July, 1918, and addressed as follows to Major R. V. Buxton, O.C., I.C.C.

Two Companies Imperial Camel Corps (Commander Maj. R. V. Buxton with sixteen officers, 300 other ranks, 400 camels, six Lewis guns) have been placed at the disposal of Hejaz Operations for the purpose of these operations on the Hejaz Railway:

(a) To seize Mudowra with the primary object of destroying the enemy's valuable water supply.

(b) To destroy the main railway bridge and tunnel at Kissela, 5 miles south of Amman, or if circumstances render (b) impracticable, which will be decided solely at the discretion of O.C., I.C.C. then

(c) To demolish the rail bridge north of Jurf ad Derwish and destroy the enemy's supply dumps and wells at Jurf station.

All operations will be night attacks. Precise plan to be decided by O.C., I.C.C. after personal reconnaissance of the positions. Stress is laid on the value of surprise, the Turks in the Hejaz being hitherto unaccustomed to attack by night. Artillery support during the operation against Mudowra will be provided by the Hejaz ten-pounder section. This section will not proceed east of the Railway but will return to Guweira. Bombing support by aeroplanes of the Hejaz Flight. Ground/air signal code to be agreed at Akaba. For the operation against Kissela, a detachment of armoured cars to be held in readiness to cover the retirement of the column to Bair in the event of pursuit by hostile cavalry from Amman. SUPPLIES: O.C. Troops, Hejaz to arrange dumps, at Rumm, 5 days rations for men and forage for animals, at El Jefer, 4 days rations and forage and at Bair, 14 days rations and forage. WATER: plentiful drinking water for men and camels at Rumm, Mudowra, Jefer, Bair, Wadi Dakhl. MEDICAL: A casualty hamla with cacolets for 12 sitting and 12 lying cases to accompany column organised by Maj. Marshall M.C., R.A.M.C. Scheme for evacuation of casualties to be prepared by Maj. Marshall. AMMUNITION: 260 S.A.A. per man, 2000 rounds per Lewis gun will be carried. EXPLOSIVES: An explosive hamla with 2500 lbs. of gun-cotton will accompany column from Akaba to Mudowra and return to Akaba. For the

Kissela operation, a hamla with 6000 lbs. of gun-cotton will meet column at Bair. GUIDES: O.C. Northern Hejaz will arrange, through Sherif Feisal, guides from the Amran Howeitat to conduct the column to Rumm. A suitable Sherif, selected by Sherif Feisal (if available Sherif Hazaar or Sherif Fahad), with guides from the Abu Tayi will join column at Rumm and conduct from thence to Mudowra and then to El Jefer. Guides from Jefer to Kissela will be arranged, on his arrival, by Lt. Col. Lawrence. ATTACHED OFFICERS: Political Officer for liaison with Arabs: Maj. Marshall R.A.M.C. (in addition to duties as M.O.). Demolitions: Capt. Scott Higgins or Bimbashi Peake, E.A. *Staff Officer* as far as Jefer only: Maj. Stirling D.S.O., M.C.

The station at Mudowra was covered by three Redoubts, the Northern, Central and Southern and, apart from medical services under Major Marshall and H.Q. under Major Buxton, the assault column was divided into six parties of which two were to sever the telegraph line and blow up the rails a mile or so to the north and south of the station. Of the remainder one party under Captain Lyall, who was awarded the M.C. for his part in the action, was to attack the Southern Redoubt, another under Lieutenant W. T. Davies of No. 10 Company, who was also awarded the M.C., was to attack and capture the main station buildings and blockhouses, another under Captain Bell-Irving of No. 7 Company was to attack the Central Redoubt, and a small raiding party under a subaltern of No. 7 Company was to create a diversion in front of the strongly held Northern Redoubt while the other parties attacked from the rear.

The assault started with a demonstration from the west to confuse the enemy and signals from the demolition parties. Then at 4 a.m. assaults were launched against the station and Southern Redoubt. Davies and his party crawled round the stone buildings throwing Mills bombs through the windows before going in with their bayonets, and very soon captured the position. The Turkish trumpeter was shot just as he was raising the instrument to his lips to sound the alarm. (Davies still has the trumpet which was sounded to call the guests to dinner at a recent Camel Corps reunion.) The attack on the Southern Redoubt was equally successful. Crouching under the sangars the assault party threw their bombs over into the Turks, many of whom were still asleep, before also going in with their bayonets. One of the casualties sustained by No. 10 Company during this attack was Lieutenant J. W. Jones who was killed. By first light the Central Redoubt had also been captured by Captain Bell-Irving and his party, but the Northern Redoubt was still putting up a stout resistance, and it was not subdued until it was bombed from the air, as described by Moore. Most of the Turkish gunners had been killed at their posts. In the meantime the Lewis gunners had fixed up a captured heavy machine gun on the flat station roof and a Turkish patrol, coming from the south to investigate the failure of Mudowra to reply to any signals, was greeted with bursts of fire from their own guns. Before it had time to recover its wits some of the assault party grabbed their rifles, jumped on their camels, which had been off saddled, and literally galloped out bareback to round up the bewildered Turks and bring them in as prisoners.

While all this was going on Major Marshall had set up an aid post in what seemed to be an old Roman Temple. During the day messages had to be ' run ' and Moore, who was in charge of signals ' borrowed ' the Turkish Commandant's Arab stallion to speed things up a bit. Just before the attack on the Northern Redoubt some delay had been caused by the apparent inability on the part of two of the signallers, newly trained and a little inexperienced, to give the correct messages from the station, which was now being used by Buxton as his H.Q., for the aerial bombing raid to begin. One of Moore's signallers, Corporal Fox, volunteered to go over himself to see what was causing the holdup. Although the intervening 300 yards or so was quite flat and swept by enemy machine gun fire he made the crossing unhurt and within seconds his messages were coming through and Moore was able to pass on the order ' Bomb Northern Redoubt '.

There is no doubt that the capture and destruction of Mudowra was a great achievement. Captain Gilman, who was in command of the Hejaz Armoured Car Battery, has related how Feisal was so delighted with the victory that he decided to give a special celebration for the Camel Corps at Jefer, where he and Lawrence were waiting to greet them on their return. A large bonfire of brushwood was collected and at the appointed time Feisal, Lawrence and all the British officers took up their positions on rugs and the ' orgy ' began. It was a sort of war dance by the Arabs, who dashed through the flames rolling over and over round the fire to the accompaniment of rhythmic chanting and firing of rifles in the air, until finally they had worked themselves up into a frenzy. Of course, there was a great feast which continued for hours after Feisal had decided that it was time for him and his guests to retire from the scene. Gilman could hear from his tent the celebration going on into the small hours which, he was told, was a most exceptional occurrence and a great honour to the guests. Even Lawrence said that he had never before witnessed such a spectacle in Arabia, and it was really put on for the benefit of the British as the victors of an operation in which the Arabs had not themselves taken any part. Among his decorations Gilman, who had originally gone to France with the H.A.C. in September, 1914, was awarded the Order of el Nahda by Feisal's father, the old King Hussein, for his services during the Hejaz campaign.

In *Seven Pillars of Wisdom* Lawrence paid many tributes to the Camel Corps of which the following is an outstanding example.

In this fashion we would gain three miles on the British, look for a plot of grass or juicy thorns, lie in the warm freshness of air, and let our beasts graze while we were overtaken; and a beautiful sight the Camel Corps would be as it came up.

Through the mirage of heat which flickered over the shining flintstones of the ridge we would see, at first, only the knotted brown mass of the column, swaying in the haze. As it grew nearer the masses used to divide into little groups, which swung; parting and breaking into one another. At last, when close to us, we would distinguish the individual riders, like great water-birds breast-deep in the silver mirage, with Buxton's athletic, splendidly mounted figure leading his sunburnt, laughing, khaki men.

It was odd to see how diversely they rode. Some sat naturally, despite the clumsy saddle; some pushed out their hinder-parts, and leaned forward like Arab villagers; others lolled in the saddle as if they were Australian riding horses. My men, judging by the look, were inclined to scoff. I told them how from that three hundred I would pick forty fellows who would out-ride, out-fight and out-suffer any forty men in Feisal's army.

High praise indeed from one who, when he did not approve of anybody or anything, never hesitated to speak his mind.

Author's note. Captain Lyall, who lives at Stamford in Lincolnshire, is believed to be the senior surviving officer of the Imperial Camel Corps Assault Column which was loaned by General Allenby to Lawrence in 1918 for the operations against the Hejaz Railway described in this chapter. In the years immediately prior to and after the 1914–1918 War he established a great reputation as a Point-to-Point and Steeple-chase rider. One of his brothers was the trainer at Bourne and another rode Grackle to win the Grand National in 1931.

Chapter Fifteen

THE END OF THE IMPERIAL CAMEL CORPS

THE HEJAZ operations brought to an end the activities of that truly extraordinary institution known as the Imperial Camel Corps, although it was not until the spring of 1919 that it was finally disbanded by which time, of course, the war had been over for several months.

The Australian and New Zealand companies had already been broken up when Colonel Buxton and his men went down to Akaba to join up with Lawrence, but remnants of the five British companies stayed on until the process of demobilisation was complete.

I should like to say once more that my story has been concerned almost exclusively with the 2nd Battalion, and it is only fair to pay my tribute to the Australians and New Zealanders who greatly distinguished themselves in many engagements at which no units of the 2nd Battalion were present. Their adventures have been recounted in other books besides Oliver Hogue's *The Cameliers* including *With the Cameliers in Palestine* by John Robertson and *The Fighting Cameliers* by Frank Reid which were published in New Zealand and Australia respectively, but as far as I am aware, nothing had been recorded or rather published, officially or unofficially, of the part played by the British during those three eventful years until I wrote my first book *Camels and Others* which had the effect of bringing to my notice from many different sources so much additional material that I was emboldened to write a second book on the same subject.

I am indeed grateful for all the assistance I have been given by some of the survivors from those far distant desert campaigns, and without which neither I nor anybody else could have completed the record. There has been no regimental history because there was no regiment. The Camel Corps never at any time had any headquarters or organisation in this country for the simple reason that all who served with it were only on detachment from their various regiments, to which they reverted automatically the moment their services for any reason came to an end, unless they were posted elsewhere.

It will, I hope, be understood that without an official record to fall back on it has been a difficult task to try and reconstruct, after so long an interval, the story as it unfolded and the background against which it has to be set. In fact there was more than one background. A glance at the map will show the vast area over which the operations of the Camel Corps extended —from Sollum and Siwa in the west to Baharia, Kharga and Dahkla in the south, Beersheba, Jaffa, Jerusalem and Jericho in the north and finally Amman, Akaba, Mudowra and Azrak in the east.

The engagements of the Camel Corps are shown on its War Memorial in Thames Embankment Gardens as Romani— Baharia—Mazar—Dahkla—Maghara—El Arish—Maghdaba— Rafa—Hassana—Gaza 1—Gaza 2—Sana Redoubt—Beersheba— Bir Khuweilfe—Hill 265—Amman—Jordan Valley—Mudowra —and it also records the names of all those who were killed or died of wounds or disease as follows:

1st Battalion (Australian)	7 officers	96 other ranks
2nd ,, (British)	14 ,,	86 ,, ,,
3rd ,, (Australian and New Zealand)	9 ,,	76 ,, ,,
4th ,, (Australian)	1 ,,	43 ,, ,,

M. G. Section	1	,,	5	,,	,,
Hong Kong and Singapore					
Battery (Indian)	1	,,	8	,,	,,
Which makes a total of	33	,,	314	,,	,,

and there must, I suppose, have been at least as many who were wounded but survived.

I cannot speak for the others but, in the 2nd Battalion, in addition to Colonel Buxton who received the D.S.O., at least eight and possibly ten officers were awarded the M.C., and a number of D.C.Ms and M.M.s were also awarded to various N.C.O.s and other ranks including, in addition to Sergeant Hobbins and Corporal Freeman of No. 10 Company both of whom received the D.C.M., Sergeant-Major Guppy of No. 8 Company who also received the D.C.M., Sergeant Bolt also of No. 8 Company who received the D.C.M. and Bar in addition to his Italian decoration and Sergeant R. Coombe, Lance Corporal W. Murray and Private R. Mills, all of No. 7 Company who with Sergeant Morgan and Private Robinson, both attached to Battalion H.Q., also received the D.C.M.

I am only too regretfully aware of the fact that there must be many omissions from my story and particularly the parts of this book which relate to the experiences of others. The Battalion was a very loosely knit organisation and, unlike in France, each company often found itself operating entirely on its own, or perhaps with one other, hundreds of miles away from the rest and with very little knowledge of what they were doing. None the less we had all come from Yeomanry regiments and there was a tremendous *esprit de corps* so much so that, whether or not we earned our appellation in the ' poem ' I have quoted as the ' Curse of Egypt ' we would certainly have regarded it as a great compliment if we had, and at any rate I can truthfully say of the Camel Corps that, for better or worse, its like will never be seen again!

The last chapter came to a close two or three years later with the unveiling of the War Memorial in a quiet and secluded part of the Embankment Gardens. The ceremony, which was intensely impressive, was performed by General Sir Philip Chetwode, that great soldier who won so much renown in the Palestine campaign, and under whose overall command the Imperial Camel Corps had so often served. The very simple dedication service was conducted by the Bishop of London and a guard of honour was supplied by the Grenadier Guards.

General Chetwode, in the act of unveiling, referred to the little known and almost unrecognised services rendered by the Imperial Camel Corps in the sun-bleached wastes of the Libyan and Sinai deserts and the Hejaz and, in dedicating the Memorial to those who had made the great sacrifice, either killed in battle or the victims of cholera, malaria and dysentery, he remarked that they had come from nearly every part of the Empire and, therefore, no place could be more fitting for the creation of a monument to their memory than this little garden in the heart of its great capital, a city which was not England's alone but which was shared by every British subject as his capital city also.

Wing Commander Ashlin was one of the cameliers who were able to attend and he has described the unveiling in the following terms:

> The simple ceremony and the General's address brought back vividly to the minds of those who had been there, the scorching days in the desert, weary forced marches, lack of sleep, food and especially water, sweating smelly camels and the remembrance of those gallant men whose memory was being honoured on that bright cold November day. The clear notes of the Last Post, sounding out above the noise of traffic in that ultra civilised metropolis, gave the final touch to a scene which those of us who were present will never forget.

I do not think that there is anything more to say.

Epilogue

LAWRENCE—AN APPRECIATION

WHAT IS there to say about Lawrence that has not been said already? He was a legend during his lifetime and has remained one since his death. I do not believe that any other man could have achieved what he so brilliantly succeeded in doing when, in the face of every conceivable difficulty, he built up and for two years co-ordinated and controlled a force of Arab guerillas, made up from dozens of different tribes many of which had for generations been enemies with blood feuds going back to God knows when. Not only that. His tremendous qualities of intellect, endurance and sheer physical courage, his determination and ability, though built on frail lines, to take his share and more than his share in the hardships imposed on him and his Arab companions by the conditions under which they lived and fought in that stark, relentless desert, almost made him a god in their eyes. Sensitive to a degree, reserved, aloof, introspective, impatient sometimes to the point of rudeness, vain sometimes to the point of arrogance, though seeking no personal glory and persistent in his refusal of all honours, basically unsure of himself and of a deeply melancholy disposition, I have never ceased to wonder how he managed first to become and then to remain for so long the venerated leader of those fierce and savage desert warriors with whom, one would think, he could never have had anything in common, but in whose company he learnt to live and endure and suffer as though he had himself been born and bred in the harsh environment from which they sprang.

Of course, like all great men, he had his detractors both before and after his publication of *Seven Pillars*. No doubt some of these were genuinely disturbed by his flamboyance, but others were actuated by nothing more or less than jealousy of the tremendous world wide publicity which he received, particularly after the famous lectures given after the war by the American reporter Lowell Thomas, who has pointed out that he did not 'invent' the Lawrence legend, nor (as was stated at the time in an English newspaper) go to Arabia in search of a myth that would sell in America, but because he had been introduced to Lawrence in Jerusalem and told by Allenby himself that it would be an excellent idea if he were to visit Arabia and then tell the world what had been happening in that remote desert.

But the cruellest attack of all came from the pen of Richard Aldington, who as late as 1955, twenty years after Lawrence's death, wrote and published a book called *Lawrence of Arabia*, which in the words of the *Oxford Companion to English Literature* was a 'bitter denigration of T. E. Lawrence and his career'. Why the bitterness I wonder and for that matter why wait for twenty years? Aldington was a novelist, biographer and poet, whose chief work was probably *Death of a Hero*, published in 1929, and based presumably on his own experiences with the army in France during the war. I have no idea whether Aldington ever met Lawrence or what triggered off this attack on his memory after all that time, but it may be that he was incensed by the limelight afforded to Lawrence, both before and after his death, as compared with the relative obscurity in which so many of his friends had fought and died in France. But although it is opportunity which makes the man I do not think that Aldington would have made much more success as a guerrilla leader in Arabia than Lawrence would have achieved as a regimental officer in France.

Seven Pillars, apart from the sheer excitement of the narrative, is not a very easy book to read and it may be that at times Lawrence drew a little on his imagination. Whether he did so, and if so to what extent, in his account of the flogging and other dreadful experiences which he was forced to endure at the hands of the Turkish Bey, nobody will ever know because there were none to witness that dreadful scourging and humiliation of the body and spirit. But that the encounter did indeed take place and inflict a permanent and ineradicable scar on Lawrence cannot be doubted for a moment.

The incident was portrayed in the film *Lawrence of Arabia* directed by David Lean, and with Peter O'Toole taking the name part, as well as certain other incidents, the authenticity of which I am inclined to question. Although O'Toole gave a virtuoso performance there was a certain unreality about it, because he seemed to tower over all the other actors, whereas Lawrence was a very small and slightly built man. Nor was he anything like the sadistic creature he was sometimes made out to be. I suppose that most men have a streak of sadism in them which may manifest itself in times of stress, and especially of war, but whatever cruelty, if any, Lawrence may have on occasion perpetrated on the enemy was as nothing compared with the suffering which he inflicted on himself.

No—this was indeed a great man, and although the suggestion has been made by some of his critics that Allenby, who was venerated by the British who served under him in Palestine just as Lawrence was by his Arabs, did not like him and could not get on with him, I can only say that this is not borne out by the tributes which Allenby paid to his memory after his death and which made it abundantly clear that he held him in the highest admiration, affection and esteem.

I have no personal knowledge of Lawrence in the sense that, so far as I am aware I never met him either in Palestine, or when I was at Oxford and he was a Fellow of All Souls, but let me repeat some words of Laurence Moore who, as already recounted, not only knew him but for a time became his close companion in the desert campaign.

And then his untimely death. And after that his detractors with their criticisms and condemnation and their claim that there was no military value in his performance. They accused him of being theatrical. Yes, looking back, the whole campaign was slightly theatrical. It had to be to impress the Arabs to say nothing of the Turks. He has also been accused of being a charlatan and poseur but I can affirm that he was neither, but a genuine performer, and I can say this as one who for one Act at least, and in a very minor role, appeared on stage with him, and that whenever we of the Imperial Camel Corps who still survive meet together to reminisce about the past, those of us who took part in the campaign are proud to recall that at one time, and a long time ago, we had the honour to serve with Lawrence in Arabia.

It was not until after I had written the preceding paragraphs that I saw a copy of the new enlarged edition of Lowell Thomas's book *With Lawrence in Arabia*, which was originally published in 1924. The importance, to me at any rate, of the new edition, which was published in the U.S.A. in 1967, lies in the Foreword and also in the Epilogue which contains a report on the men around Lawrence and, although it had not been my intention to become involved too deeply in the attacks which have been made on Lawrence ever since his death, but which have only reached their climax in recent years, I feel that I cannot altogether escape it, and I am more than grateful to Lowell Thomas for allowing me to make use of some of the material which his book contains.

At the same time I have made no alterations to the words which I have already written and which, at any rate so far as the film is concerned, appear to coincide very closely with the views expressed by many of those, including the late Sir Basil Liddell Hart, who were closely acquainted with Lawrence and are far better qualified, therefore, to judge than myself, and it is significant that while they unanimously agree that the film was a brilliant technical achievement, and the photography superb, they also affirm in no uncertain terms that the story which it told and the delineation of the principal characters, such as Allenby and Lawrence, which it portrayed, bore scarcely any resemblance to the real facts.

I suppose that there has never been such a controversial motion picture and that the reason for this is that there has never been quite such a controversial figure as Lawrence himself. None the less I am convinced that, when the final history is written, the attacks on his reputation and achievements will be forgotten, and he will be acclaimed as one of the greatest figures of his age.

Lowell Thomas has stated in his book that in his opinion the main reasons for these attacks are threefold, (1) because some of the British officers of the so-called Mesopotamian group believed that they should have had the support that went to Lawrence, and resented his efforts on behalf of the Hejaz Arabs, (2) because of the bitter Near and Middle Eastern clash of interest between the British and the French Empires, and (3) because of the simple fact that Lawrence was in truth a great man.

The last of these may appear to be a little fanciful but Lowell Thomas relates how on the eve of the publication of Richard Aldington's book he told Lord Beaverbrook, who was passing through New York on his way back to London, that he had received information to the effect that a British novelist was about to bring out a smear book on Lawrence and that his friends were concerned, to which Beaverbrook replied, 'Don't worry. It will simply add to Lawrence's stature. Every great man is subject to ------------ attack. There are no exceptions. The one who will suffer will be the author of the book.'

As to the second reason there can be no doubt whatever that such a clash existed, and it must be admitted that Lawrence can hardly have endeared himself to the French by his continuing

and outspoken hostility towards them, while the French in their
turn regarded him also as an enemy and as the man chiefly
responsible for spoiling their plans of a Middle Eastern Empire.
Incidentally it has to be remembered that Richard Aldington
was an ardent Francophile, who had lived in France for years,
and it is easy to understand the influence which his French friends
brought to bear on him, and which may have been a principal
factor in the cruel attack which he made on Lawrence.

As for the Mesopotamian group there is undoubtedly truth
in the statement that criticism of Lawrence originally came
from those who were involved in the Mesopotamian campaign,
but Lowell Thomas goes out of his way to point out that there
were exceptions to the general rule and that some of these were
to remain Lawrence's lifelong friends.

Inevitably there was another group from which Lawrence
might have expected very little sympathy or understanding,
the Zionists, and it is worthy of note that this included a very
senior member of Allenby's staff, who after the war said of
Lawrence, 'He owes everything he has ever had to Allenby.
He was created by Allenby, and his reputation, *such as it is*, is of
Allenby's creation.' (The italics are mine.)

And yet Chaim Weizmann, the great Zionist leader and
' father of modern Israel' said this, ' There was a lasting friend-
ship between us. I frequently had occasion to ask his advice
. . . Lawrence readily gave not only this but his personal help
in furthering both the Zionist aspirations *and an understanding
with the Arabs* . . . a very great service on his part to the cause of
Zionism. . . . I remember with gratitude his help in furthering
the cause of the Jewish people.' (Again the italics are mine.)

It stands to reason that the controversy, for so long as it
continues, will lie between those who were more or less
Lawrence's contemporaries, including the men who accompanied
him on the long and bitter desert marches which he and others
have described so well, who fought by his side, who knew and

understood him and the tasks which he had set himself to perform, who for one reason or another became associated with
him both during and after the war, who marvelled at his achievements, or who were simply his friends, on the one hand, and the
increasing number of people who never knew him, who were
perhaps not even born when he led and inspired his Arabs
throughout the vicissitudes and privations of that amazing war,
and whose writings are based on the so-called fresh documentary
evidence which they have succeeded in bringing to light, on
the other hand.

To illustrate what the first of these groups thought about
Lawrence here are a few of the quotations given by Lowell
Thomas from men whose views can hardly be described as
other than worthy of respect, and all of whom are dead.

Lord Wavell (who had been a major on Allenby's staff)
' His name will live in history. He had many fairy godmothers
at his cradle, with gifts of fearlessness, of understanding, of a
love of learning, of craftsmanship, of humour, of spartan
endurance, of frugality, of selflessness.'

Lord Lloyd (who went on special missions to the Hejaz)
' On the long night marches we had wonderful talks . . . his
brain is like quicksilver and his humour unquenchable . . . I
have got very fond of him, and respect his indomitable courage,
self sacrifice and enterprise. Alone he has conquered this
country.'

Colonel W. F. Stirling (who was Chief of Staff to Colonel P. C.
Joyce, who was in command of British co-operation with the
Arabs)
' Lawrence was the greatest genius England has produced in
the last two centuries.'

Liman von Sanders (the German General who commanded the
Turkish and German armies in Gallipoli and later in Palestine)

'The desert revolt was a British success, because of the immense handicap it imposed on the Turks. With courage, endurance and skill Lawrence captured the support not only of the Arabs, but of Allenby.'

Lord Winterton (who remained behind with Lawrence after the Imperial Camel Corps Assault Column was withdrawn from the Hejaz)

'A noteworthy feature of the campaign was the personality of Lawrence. At intervals, attacks by men of lesser minds are made upon his reputation and claim to fame. These blandly ignore the regard for him felt by so many men of eminence who knew him and, in many cases, worked with him. They include Winston Churchill, Bernard Shaw, Allenby, Wavell, Trenchard, Storrs and others. They brush aside the admiration which we, who served with him, had for his genius and the great influence which he had over our Arab allies. I have worked directly under many eminent men. Of these, in my judgement, only Churchill exceeds Lawrence in stature. . . .'

And finally *Sir Winston Churchill* himself (who in 1921 was Colonial Secretary and succeeded after several attempts in persuading Lawrence to join his newly created Middle East Department as adviser on Arab affairs. It was this Department which brought about the offer of the throne of Iraq to Feisal, who in the previous year had been driven out of Syria by the French)

'He was a dweller on the mountain tops, where the air was cold, crisp and rarefied. . . . His name will live in history, in English letters, in the annals of war, in the traditions of the Royal Air Force, in the legends of Arabia. I was under his spell and deemed myself his friend. I account him one of the greatest beings alive in our time.'

Before bringing this chapter to a close I feel that I must make some reference to the book *The Secret Lives of Lawrence of Arabia*, by Phillip Knightley and Colin Simpson, which has been published recently.

The authors have certainly carried out a wonderful task of investigation and, although they have succeeded in bringing to light certain documentary evidence, part of which on the face of it would not appear to redound to Lawrence's credit, I detect that they are by no means wholly unsympathetic towards him or unmindful of the almost insoluble problems which confronted him towards the end of and immediately after the war.

There are just four comments which I, as a staunch supporter and admirer of Lawrence, would like to make on the story which they have unfolded.

1. Lawrence did not create a policy entirely on his own. He was, after all, acting under orders from higher authority with whom, it is hardly necessary to add, he frequently disagreed. I am not, of course, referring to Allenby, with whom he succeeded in establishing a firm and lasting relationship based on mutual respect, but to his superiors in London.

2. The authors confirm that one of his main motivations throughout the Revolt, apart from patriotism, was hatred of the French and their ambitions to create for themselves an empire in the Middle East. I have already mentioned the fact that the French were equally bitter in their attitude towards Lawrence. There was not only a constant clash of personalities but also an issue, which became increasingly aggravated with the approach of final victory and the complete destruction of the Turkish Empire, and which involved nothing more or less than the political reorganisation after the war of the vast territories which had been wrested from Turkish domination. It is easy to say that there was nothing in the extension of either the British or the French interests in the Middle East which was likely to help or at any rate cement the cause of Arab independence, and it may well be that the Arabs had been promised,

in return for their assistance, a far greater degree of autonomy than they were ever likely to achieve in the forseeable future, but the plan which Lawrence had gradually been evolving in his mind, and for which he fought so hard during the Paris Peace Conference, would have gone a long way towards meeting Arab aspirations. However, the plan was overruled and in the result the French were given the protectorate over Syria and the Lebanon, both of which Feisal had rightly or wrongly imagined were to be handed to him.

But the blame for this deception, if deception there was, lay not so much with Lawrence as with the British Government. It originated with the famous—or infamous—Sykes-Picot agreement, a secret Anglo-French arrangement which was concluded in 1916 and provided that after the war Britain, France and Russia (which had been a party to the negotiations) should have well defined spheres of influence over various parts of the vast territories which Turkey would be compelled to relinquish following the break up of the Ottoman Empire. These included Palestine, the whole of Mesopotamia (now Iraq) except for its northern district of Mosul, and what is now Jordan for the British, Syria including the Lebanon, and Mosul for the French, and the Caucasus for the Russians. It is doubtful whether Lawrence knew anything about this agreement at the time and in fact it was not until Russia for its own reasons let the cat out of the bag at the end of 1917 that its existence was revealed to the world. Whether or not it would ever have been disclosed to the Arabs until it was too late to retract is a matter for speculation, and the only accusation which can be levelled against Lawrence is that after it came to his knowledge, as it was obviously bound to do, he continued to persuade Feisal that it was the firm intention of the British that the Arabs should be granted their independence. By then, however, Lawrence had been placed in an almost impossible position and in any case he was determined to do his utmost to wreck the Sykes-Picot agreement which he detested from the start and which cut right across his own grandiose plan for the establishment, admittedly under British protection, of a semi-independent Arab state which would include in addition to Northern Arabia the whole of Mesopotamia, Jordan and Syria, with the possible exception of the Lebanon which might have to go to the French.

3. What the original intention of Lawrence and, for that matter the British Government as well, may have been as regards Palestine it is difficult to determine but, with the announcement in November, 1917, by Mr Balfour, the Foreign Secretary, of his famous Declaration that H.M. Government viewed with favour the establishment in Palestine of a national home for the Jewish people, any hope which Feisal may have entertained, whether justifiably or not, that Palestine was to come within the area of Arab independence must have been shattered overnight.

Feisal was indeed, as the authors point out, desperately short of money after the war and it was Lawrence's idea that arrangements should be made for him to be financed on a large scale by international Jewry. According to what Lawrence said at the Peace Conference, Feisal who, not unnaturally, took the view that he was entitled to make his own choice as to who should be his financial advisers, and preferred to obtain the assistance of British or American Zionists in this capacity, had stated that the Zionists would be acceptable to the Arabs ' on terms '. What these were to be is not exactly clear but even as early as June, 1918, there had been a meeting between Feisal and Dr Chaim Weizmann who, according to his own account, told him that, if he wanted to build up a strong and prosperous Arab Kingdom, it was the Jews and only the Jews who would be able to help him. They would be his neighbours and would not represent any danger to him as they were not and never would be a great power. The authors go on to say that at a subsequent meeting in London between Feisal, Weizmann and

Lawrence just before the Peace Conference, Weizmann explained that, in accordance with the Zionist programme, the Conference should recognise the national and historical right of the Jews to Palestine, that Britain should be the Trustee power, that the Jews should have an adequate share in government and that the country should be developed so as to create room for 4,000,000 or 5,000,000 Jews without encroaching on the ownership rights of the Arab peasantry. In return the Jews would be prepared to render Feisal every assistance in brains and money in order to help revive his country. An agreement was actually signed along these lines, Feisal making a reservation about the Arabs obtaining their independence as demanded in a memorandum he had submitted to the Foreign Office.

Now it may well be that, so far as Lawrence was concerned, his chief motivation was to set in motion a series of events which would have had the result of pushing the French out of Syria because, with a Zionist centre established in Jerusalem and the willingness and ability of the Zionists, in return for concessions, to provide Feisal with all the financial assistance he so badly needed, no help would be required from the French, and there would be no need, therefore, to grant them any concessionary rights over Syria. None the less the position of Feisal would have been considerably strengthened by the addition of Syria to his Kingdom and I cannot see why the suggestion should be made that Lawrence was acting with a cynical disregard for Feisal's interests. The complete independence of the Arabs might or might not be achieved in the course of time but, for the immediate future, Lawrence was able to see that the establishment of a Zionist state in Palestine was not necessarily inimical to the interests of the Arabs as a whole. Quite the contrary in fact, because the union between the Zionists and Arabia, the latter supplying the land and the former the money, would have brought considerable benefits to both.

To the question, therefore, posed by the authors as to what

the shape of the Middle East would have been today had such a scheme succeeded I would unhesitatingly reply, 'It might have been much better and it could not possibly have been any worse.'

4. A discussion of Lawrence's private life is really outside the scope of this book and I propose to say very little on the subject. Like all great men he had his share, and perhaps more than his share, of human foibles but whether or not he had homosexual tendencies seems to me to be as entirely irrelevant as it is still unproven. As far as the incident of his capture at Deraa and his debasement by the Turkish Bey are concerned I am, as I have already stated, prepared to concede that Lawrence's account of this may not be strictly accurate in detail, although I for one am convinced that in substance it is true, and I do not think that the discovery that the Bey was known in Turkey as an aggressive heterosexual or that, had he ever exhibited any homosexual leanings, he would never have been admitted to, or at any rate, lasted as a member of the first nationalist parliament at Ankara, with its puritanical overtones, really contributes very much to an assessment of Lawrence's sexual proclivities. All we do know, as the authors' researches seem to have made clear, is that whatever may have been the exact experience which Lawrence suffered on that dreadful occasion, he was never able to heal the wound which it had inflicted on his psyche and which, I think, goes far to explain what happened, or is supposed to have happened, to him later on.

Robert Graves has pointed out that Lawrence is on record as having stated that, long before the war, he had fallen in love with a woman in Damascus who, throughout the desert campaign, was never for a minute absent from his waking thoughts and who provided a disproportionate share of the motive for the Arabian adventure. He has gone on to say that in Lawrence's dedication to *Seven Pillars of Wisdom* she is addressed as S.A., which has been mistaken for her initials, or those of Sheikh

Achmed, a close Arab friend, or even of a country—Saudi Arabia—but which in fact, according to hints subsequently dropped by Lawrence, stood for ' Son Altesse ', the language of the troubadour for the lady who gave him inspiration to write his poems, and devotion to whom sustained him through perils and hardships when he went on crusade. Fact or fantasy? I doubt if we shall ever know, but it is all part of the romance and mystique which will for ever be associated with that enigmatic, tortured, but somehow noble figure ' Lawrence of Arabia '.

INDEX